MINERALS AND ROCKS

MINERALS
AND ROCKS

KEITH LYE

Consultant
Paul Henderson

Kingfisher Books

First published in 1979.
This edition published in 1985 by Kingfisher Books Limited
Elsley Court, 20 – 22 Great Titchfield Street, London W1P 7AD
A Grisewood & Dempsey Company

Reprinted 1986

BRITISH LIBRARY CATALOGUING IN PUBLICATION DATA
Lye, Keith
    Minerals and rocks. – (Kingfisher guides)
    1. Mineralogy   2. Rocks – Identification
    I. Title
    549   QE366.8
    ISBN 0 86272 138 5

Colour separations by Newsele Litho, Milan, London
Printed and bound in Italy by Vallardi Industrie
Grafiche, Milan

CONTENTS

INTRODUCTION

Minerals and rocks have been of great importance to Man since the dawn of human history. In the early Stone Age, people began to make flint and obsidian tools. They found that these rocks had naturally sharp edges when they were fractured. They also learned how to sharpen other rocks and minerals. Around 10,000 years ago, people discovered how to make copper implements and, 5000 years later, they found out how to make bronze from copper and tin. The invention of bronze, a harder metal than copper, marked the end of the Stone Age. But even more important was the discovery, about 3300 years ago, of how to work iron. Iron, a tough metal, is more common than copper and tin, and the Iron Age marked the start of modern times.

Interest in the Earth's riches was not confined to minerals and rocks used in technology. People were also fascinated by the beauty of minerals. Gold was first used for jewellery in the Stone Age, and silver came into use in the Bronze Age. By the time of the ancient Greeks, many minerals were in use. The modern names of some minerals come from Greek words. For example, the name nephrite (greenstone) comes, oddly enough, from the Greek word *nephros*, meaning kidney. It received this name because the Greeks believed that the wearer of a nephrite amulet had protection against kidney complaints. The Greeks also thought that amethysts prevented drunkenness and the Greek word *amethystos* means unintoxicated. Many other magical beliefs surrounded minerals. For example, rock crystal, a kind of quartz, was supposed to prevent tooth-ache and internal bleeding.

What are Minerals and Rocks?

People sometimes talk of minerals and rocks as though they were the same things. However, both terms have precise meanings. First, minerals are naturally-occurring, *inorganic* (lifeless) substances. Coal, oil and natural gas are not minerals, because they are *organic* (formed from once-living matter). They are usually called *fossil fuels*. Minerals consist of elements, substances that cannot be broken down into other substances by chemical means. Some minerals consist of one element. But, commonly, they are chemical combinations of two or more elements (see page 34). Each mineral has a definite composition and any part of a mineral is the same as any other part. Rocks are composed of mineral grains, but the proportions of minerals vary from one sample to another. Sometimes, as in limestone, a rock is composed mostly of one mineral, but most rocks consist of two, three or more minerals. Rocks need not be solid. Sand, peat and mud are rocks to geologists.

The 'Temple of Osiris' in Bryce National Park, Utah, USA.

January	February	March	
Garnet Faithfulness	Amethyst Sincerity	Aquamarine Courage	Bloodstone

April	May	June	
Diamond Innocence	Emerald Love	Pearl Health	Alexandrite natural light / artificial light

July	August	September
Ruby Contentment	Peridot Sardonyx Married Happiness	Sapphire Clear Thinking

October	November	December
Opal Tourmaline Hope	Topaz Citrine Fidelity	Turquoise Zircon Prosperity

Birthstones are gems that symbolize the month of a person's birth. In the Middle Ages, many people thought that each gem represented a particular quality, such as faithfulness, sincerity, and so on. They also believed that birthstones brought good luck and influenced the personality of the wearer.

The Composition of the Earth

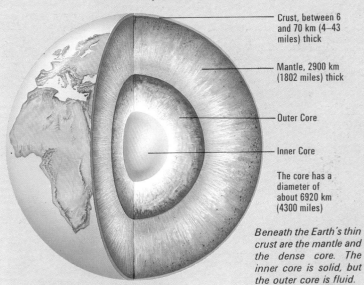

Crust, between 6 and 70 km (4–43 miles) thick

Mantle, 2900 km (1802 miles) thick

Outer Core

Inner Core

The core has a diameter of about 6920 km (4300 miles)

Beneath the Earth's thin crust are the mantle and the dense core. The inner core is solid, but the outer core is fluid.

Peridotite

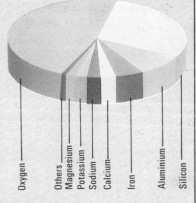

Oxygen | Others | Magnesium | Potassium | Sodium | Calcium | Iron | Aluminium | Silicon

The Earth's mantle is denser than the crust. It may be composed, in part, of a heavy dark rock called peridotite, above. Above right: The diagram shows that oxygen and silicon are the chief elements in the crust. By weight, oxygen makes up 46·60 per cent and silicon 27·72 per cent. Aluminium, iron, calcium, sodium, potassium and magnesium make up 24·27 per cent. Other elements add up to 1·41 per cent.

Left: Tremendous forces in the Earth squeeze rock layers into folds. Opposite: The diagram shows that the crust is split into moving plates. In the oceans, the oceanic ridges form plate edges, where new rock is being added to the crust as molten magma rises from the upper mantle. This pushes the plates apart. In places, plate edges are forced downwards. Rocks in the descending plate melt. The molten material may rise again through volcanoes.

Inside the Earth

Before we can study minerals and rocks, we must first know something about the composition of the Earth. The Earth is divided into three zones: the crust, mantle and core. (The core itself consists of a liquid outer part and a solid inner part.) The chief difference between the zones is their density. The upper mantle is about $1\frac{1}{4}$ times as dense as the continents, which explains why the continents do not sink into the mantle. And the core is about 4–5 times as dense as the crust. We do not know for certain what minerals and rocks are in the mantle and core. But scientists believe that the upper mantle may contain such heavy rocks as peridotite (see the picture on page 11). This rock appears occasionally on the surface, but it is denser than most other crustal rocks. Scientists think that it may have been brought up from the mantle by tremendous Earth movements.

The Earth's core is extremely dense and it probably consists largely of heavy substances, such as iron and nickel. This theory is supported by evidence from meteorites, some of which are light and stony, while others are composed of nickel-iron. Some geologists consider that the stony meteorites may be crustal material, while nickel-iron meteorites may be fragments of core material. For a description of meteorites, see page 122.

Composition of the Crust

Because so little is known of the mantle and core, the study of minerals and rocks is confined mostly to the Earth's thin crust. Two elements, oxygen and silicon, make up 74·32 per cent of the weight of the crust. Other common elements are aluminium (8·13 per cent), iron (5·00 per cent), calcium (3·63 per cent), sodium (2·83 per cent), potassium (2·59 per cent) and magnesium (2·09 per cent). Hence, although 92 elements occur naturally in the crust, eight account for 98·59 per cent of the crust's total weight.

Moving Continents

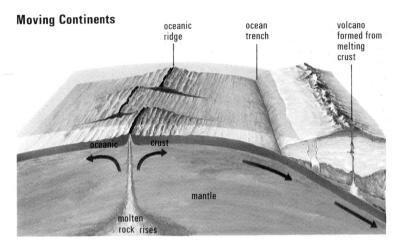

oceanic ridge

ocean trench

volcano formed from melting crust

oceanic crust

mantle

molten rock rises

Of these eight elements, only iron is found on its own as a native element (see page 58). The others only occur naturally in combination with other elements. Mineralogists have identified nearly 3000 minerals. The commonest are the silicates, which are so-called because they are essentially combinations of silicon and oxygen, often with one or more of the six other abundant elements. Common silicates include feldspar minerals, quartz, the micas, olivines, pyroxenes and amphiboles (see pages 82–101). These minerals occur widely in many rocks. For example, the familiar rock granite consists essentially of feldspars and quartz, together with micas or other silicate minerals. Because they are so much more common than other minerals, geologists call these silicates *rock-forming minerals*. This distinguishes them from other minerals, which occur in comparatively small amounts. The only major rock-forming minerals which are not silicates are the carbonates, particularly calcite and dolomite (see page 77). Carbonates form rocks called limestones and dolomites (see pages 114–5).

The Changing Earth

To understand the origin of minerals and rocks, we must remember that our planet Earth is subject to constant change. The crust was first formed from hot molten material, called *magma*. In the early days of Earth history, magma must have covered most of the surface. When the magma cooled and hardened, minerals were formed. These minerals together constituted rocks, which we call *igneous* rocks, after the Latin word *igneus*, meaning fire. But our planet had an atmosphere, composed of gases and water vapour released from the Earth's interior by volcanic action. Because of the atmosphere, the rocks were attacked by weathering and other natural forces, such as running water, the wind and ice. From the moment of their formation, rocks on the surface were broken down into loose fragments. These fragments were transported into seas and lakes, where they were compacted and cemented together into solid *sedimentary* rocks. But heat and pressure often transform igneous and sedimentary rocks into *metamorphic* rocks (see the chapter on *The Formation of Rocks*, pages 46–57).

Such forces are still changing the Earth's crust today. Evidence that the Earth is still active can also be seen whenever a volcano erupts or an earthquake shakes the land. Many volcanic eruptions and earthquakes are caused by continental drift. Continental drift occurs because the Earth's crust is split, like a cracked egg, into a number of rigid plates. The plates are moved around by forces in the upper mantle. For example, in the major oceans, there are long underwater mountain ranges, called oceanic ridges or rises. Along the centres of some of these ridges, new rock is forming from molten magma which is welling up from the upper mantle. The oceanic ridges are, in fact, the edges of plates, and the addition of new rock is pushing the plates apart and widening the oceans. The rate at which some plates are moving apart is about 2 cm (0·8 inches) per year.

However, our planet is not increasing in size because of the addition of this new rock. Instead, in some places, the crust is being destroyed as some plates are pushed down beneath others in a series of jerky movements. As a plate edge is forced down into the mantle, it is melted and becomes magma. This magma may return to the surface through volcanoes. Hence,

The map shows the location of important mineral ores around the world.

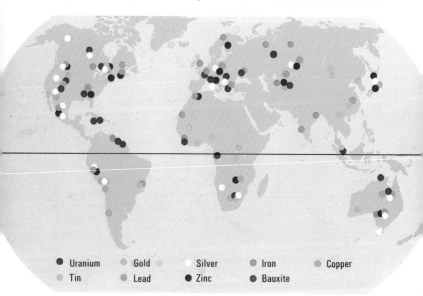

| ● Uranium | ● Gold | ● Silver | ● Iron | ● Copper |
| ● Tin | ● Lead | ● Zinc | ● Bauxite | |

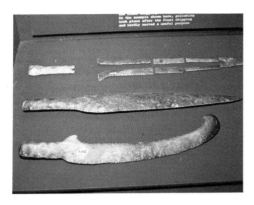

Above: A flint scythe and spearheads, made over 4000 years ago. Below: Plaster of Paris is made from a mineral, gypsum. Right: The British Royal Sceptre contains a diamond called 'The Star of Africa No 1', the world's largest cut diamond.

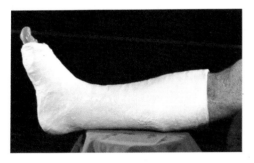

while some crustal rocks are forming on or near the surface, others are being destroyed.

Plate movements have been continuing for millions of years. Scientists think that, about 200 million years ago, all the continents were joined together as one. Plate movements have made them drift apart. As the continents drifted, so ancient oceans were closed up and new oceans were formed. In some places, where plates pushed against each other, the sediments between them were squeezed up into new fold mountains, such as the Alps, Andes and Himalayas. The sedimentary rocks in these lofty ranges contain fossils of sea organisms.

Riches of the Earth

The Earth's crust is a rich storehouse of valuable minerals and fossil fuels, although economic minerals (those that can be mined at a profit) are unevenly spread around the world (see map on page 14). Most metals come from mineral ores, which contain a sufficiently high proportion of a valuable metal to make their extraction economic. The proportion varies. For example, it is not economic to extract iron, a common metal, from ores that contain less than 30–60 per cent iron. But silver is an extremely rare metal and a silver ore may contain less than one per cent of that metal.

Minerals can occur in igneous, sedimentary and metamorphic rocks. Some minerals are being used up at a fast rate, because the demand for them has been steadily increasing. The rising demand is caused partly by the growth of the world's population and partly by the world-wide rise in people's standards of living. For example, shortages of copper, gold, lead and tin have been predicted for the early years of the 21st century. And some experts estimate that all the known reserves of oil will be used up in less than 30 years at the present rate of consumption.

To avoid serious problems, we must learn to use the Earth's resources more wisely. Scrap metal must be conserved and re-used; new ways of extracting substances from seawater must be invented; alternative materials, such as plastics, and alternative power sources must be developed; and the search for new reserves of minerals and fossil fuels must continue.

Prospecting Methods: Old and New

The discovery of minerals was once largely a matter of accident. In the 1500s, some prospectors used divining rods, which were supposed to twitch in their hands when minerals were nearby. And, until recent

Minerals, especially metals, have many uses, as can be seen in the diagram, below, which shows some of the many materials used to make a car.

Opposite: The Premier mine, near Pretoria, South Africa, is the world's largest single diamond mine. Here, miners prepare for blasting.

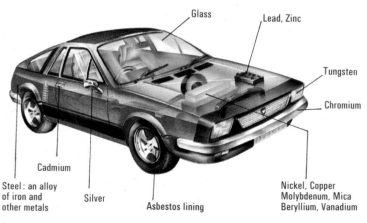

Glass

Lead, Zinc

Tungsten

Chromium

Cadmium

Steel: an alloy of iron and other metals

Silver

Asbestos lining

Nickel, Copper Molybdenum, Mica Beryllium, Vanadium

times, lonely prospectors roamed the world, examining gravel in river beds in the hunt for traces of valuable minerals. If they found, by chance, a nugget of gold, they would then search for a vein in nearby rocks from which the nugget had come. News of a rich strike spread quickly and a gold rush began.

Today, however, prospecting is much more scientific. Most prospectors are trained geologists, who know the best kinds of places to look for minerals. They are equipped with geological maps, which show surface outcrops of rocks, and often with air photographs, which reveal features not obvious on the ground. Seismology, the study of vibrations in the Earth's crust caused by earthquakes and explosions, is valuable in the search for oil. Seismologists set off small explosions in the ground. They record the paths of seismic waves through the crust on instruments called seismographs. The paths of seismic waves are bent by rocks of varying densities and a study of the results reveals underground rock structures.

Other prospecting instruments include gravimeters, which record local variations in rock densities; magnetometers, which detect minerals, such as magnetite, which have magnetic properties; and Geiger counters, which are used to locate radioactive minerals. Chemistry also comes to the aid of modern prospectors. For example, a study of the chemicals in samples of soil, water or even plants may lead prospectors to important reserves of economic minerals.

Mining
Mining was once confined to digging on or near the surface. But, today, mines can reach deep into the crust. One mine in South Africa has reached a depth of 3·8 km (nearly 2·4 miles), although most mines are

Coralline limestone, which is limestone formed from compacted coral skeletons, was used to build this ancient Mayan pyramid, in the Yucatan peninsula, in south-east Mexico.

The superb Jefferson Memorial in Washington DC, the capital of the United States, was constructed from Utah marble, a metamorphic rock. It was dedicated in 1943.

The tough igneous rock, granite, makes a fine building stone. Above: The photograph shows buildings made from local granite in old Aberdeen. Aberdeen, in north-eastern Scotland, is often called 'the granite city'. Left: The Qutub Minar, in Delhi, India, is a minaret (tower of a Muslim mosque), built from red sandstone, a sedimentary rock. It was constructed in 1193. The Qutub Minar is 72·5 metres (238 ft) high.

less than 1·8 km (1·1 miles) deep. But surface, or open-cast, mining remains generally cheaper and still accounts for most of the world's mineral production. Quarrying is a kind of surface mining. It is especially important for extracting kaolin (clay) for ceramics, and building stones, such as granite, limestone, marble, sandstone and slate. The search for minerals in alluvial deposits, such as river gravels, remains important. These deposits may contain tough or heavy minerals, such as diamond, gold or platinum.

Underground mining was once dangerous. But most modern mines are equipped with safety equipment and are well-ventilated, although accidents may still occur. Some minerals can be obtained from great depths without digging a mine. For example, halite (rock salt) and potash dissolve in water. They can be extracted in solution by water which is pumped down to the deposits and then brought back to the surface. Sulphur does not dissolve in water. But it can be mined by pumping hot steam down to the deposit. The steam melts the sulphur, which is then forced to the surface by compressed air.

Some minerals, such as galena, above, the main ore of lead, are metallic minerals. Others, such as talc, right, are non-metallic minerals.

The World of Minerals

Minerals, in all their colourful splendour, occur throughout the Earth's crust. Apart from their beauty, minerals have fascinating structures and properties. For example, some minerals have the same chemical composition, but the arrangement of their atoms and their properties are completely different; both graphite and diamond are forms of pure carbon (see pages 61–2).

The names of minerals may sound bewildering to the inexperienced. Some names refer to places where the mineral was found; andalusite was found in Andalusia, in southern Spain. Other names refer to the properties of minerals. The name rutile comes from the Latin *rutilus* (reddish), referring to the colour of the mineral. Some names are derived from people; sillimanite was named after the American geologist Benjamin Silliman.

Collecting minerals and rocks is a popular hobby. Armed with a geological hammer, a steel chisel, a bag, wrapping paper and, perhaps, a geological map of the neighbourhood, an amateur can soon build up a basic collection. To find the best specimens, however, we must know about the kinds of places where they are likely to occur.

Where Minerals Occur

Common rock-forming minerals occur widely (see page 13). For example, quartz, feldspars and micas occur in granite; calcite forms limestones; and many sands consist of quartz grains. But to find really good specimens, especially of minerals that are not silicates or carbonates, we must understand how they form.

Some fine specimens with well-developed crystals occur in igneous rocks, such as pegmatites (pages 103–4). Such minerals crystallize from mineral-rich fluids, left behind after the formation of granite. Other

Geologists search for traces of minerals in alluvial deposits. Traces in these deposits often lead geologists to valuable mineral veins.

minerals occur in veins, which range in thickness from a few centimetres to several metres. Veins are deposited from mineral-rich fluids in joints and fissures in all kinds of rocks. Those deposited from hot fluids are called *hydrothermal veins*. These veins often contain many less common minerals, especially non-silicates. The veins are often mined for ores and fine mineral specimens may be found in mine dumps. Some hydrothermal fluids replace existing rocks, such as limestones. The minerals in some veins may be altered. Altered, or *secondary*, minerals may occur near the tops of veins, where water and air have reacted with the original, or *primary*, minerals.

Other minerals form in cavities in rocks. For example, *geodes* are rounded, hollow stones, which contain crystals that grew inwards towards the centre. Geodes may contain crystals of amethyst, calcite and zeolites. *Druses* are cavities containing mineral crystals which have formed in roughly parallel bands. *Vugs* are cavities in veins, and *nodules* (also called *concretions*) form in various rocks, such as the lumps of flint found in chalk. *Amygdales* are minerals which fill cavities in igneous rocks (see page 49).

Some mineral specimens, such as garnet, are associated particularly with metamorphic rocks (see page 56). Others, such as evaporites, occur in chemical sedimentary deposits (see page 53). Alluvial deposits, as we have seen, may contain heavy minerals which have been washed out of veins. These so-called *placer deposits* may also occur in ancient sedimentary rocks.

Mineral associations are a useful guide to locating minerals. For example, anhydrite, gypsum and halite all form from evaporating seawater and so they tend to occur together. Galena and sphalerite are examples of associated minerals in hydrothermal veins. Important mineral associations are mentioned in the *Guide to Minerals* (pages 58–101).

Identifying Minerals
Collectors may come across minerals which they cannot identify. In such cases, they should seek the help of a geological museum or society. But many minerals can be identified from their properties, including hardness, specific gravity, cleavage and fracture, colour and streak, optical properties, crystal forms, chemical composition and reactiveness, and other less common features.

Hardness
Geologists use the Mohs' scale of hardness, which is explained on page 23. New collectors should practise using minerals 1–9 in the scale to work out the hardness of other minerals.

Specific Gravity
Specific gravity is the ratio between the weight of a mineral and an equal volume of water. A simple way of measuring specific gravity is shown on

Hardness

Hardness is an important characteristic of minerals. A scale of hardness was devised in 1822 by an Austrian mineralogist, Friedrich Mohs. Mohs selected 10 minerals, shown on the right. He arranged them in order of hardness, so that, for example, calcite (3) will scratch gypsum (2) but not fluorite (4). Mohs' scale runs from talc (1) to diamond (10). The intervals on the scale are not regular, although corundum (9) is roughly 9 times as hard as talc. However, diamond is about 40 times as hard as talc. Some collectors take the 10 minerals on the scale around with them to test the hardness of specimens. But one can also use everyday objects — fingernails, copper coins, glass, penknives and steel files, as shown in the diagram. The 'Guide to Minerals' (pages 58–101) gives the hardness of each mineral. When you scratch a specimen, choose an inconspicuous spot. Clean the specimen after you have tried to scratch it. This must be done because the softer mineral may leave a powder mark, which can be mistaken for a scratch.

A fingernail has a hardness of about $2\frac{1}{2}$.

A copper coin has a hardness of about $3\frac{1}{2}$.

Minerals of 6 or more will scratch glass.

A penknife ($5\frac{1}{2}$) will scratch apatite but not orthoclase.

A special steel file will scratch quartz.

Mohs' scale

1. Talc
2. Gypsum
3. Calcite
4. Fluorite
5. Apatite
6. Orthoclase
7. Quartz
8. Topaz
9. Corundum
10. Diamond

Above: These gold bars stacked in a bank vault are symbols of wealth and power. Inexperienced collectors may mistake common pyrite (iron pyrites), above right, for gold, and it is often called fool's gold. But pyrite is harder, more brittle and has a lower specific gravity than gold.

this page. It is based on Archimedes' principle, which states that any substance weighs less in a fluid than it does in the air, and that the 'lost' weight is the equivalent of the fluid it displaces. If you have a sample of gold weighing, say, 100 grams, it will weigh about 94·82 grams when immersed in water. The weight lost is 5·18 grams. The specific gravity is 100 divided by 5·18 which equals 19·3. This means that gold is 19·3 times as heavy as the same volume of water. The specific gravity of minerals ranges from 1 to about 23, but the average for all minerals is only about 2·6.

Measuring Specific Gravity

Specific gravity is the ratio between the weight of a substance and an equal volume of water. To measure specific gravity, first weigh a specimen in air, below left, and then weigh it in water, below right. The specific gravity is the weight of the specimen in air, divided by the difference between its weight in air and its weight in water.

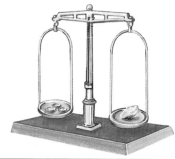
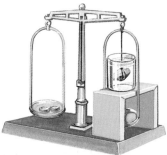

Cleavage and Fracture

Muscovite

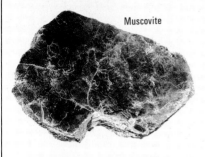

Siderite

Obsidian

Cleavage is a feature of many minerals. Perfect cleavage occurs in muscovite and siderite. Muscovite has one cleavage, called basal cleavage, because it splits into thin sheets. You can see the layers in the specimen. Siderite has perfect rhombohedral cleavage. This means that it cleaves in three directions into rhombohedra (six-sided prisms, each of whose sides is a parallelogram). Some minerals split in an irregular way, called fracture. Obsidian, right, is a rock. But it has conchoidal (shell-like) fracture, which is a characteristic of several minerals, including quartz. The curved fractured surface resembles a sea-shell.

Cleavage and Fracture

When minerals are broken apart, some split along one or more plane (flat, smooth) surfaces. This property is called cleavage. It is related to how the atoms in the mineral are *bonded* (held together). For example, mica cleaves into thin sheets, because the bonding *within* the sheets is strong, while the bonding *between* them is weak. When a mineral breaks into thin sheets, it is said to have *basal* cleavage. Some minerals have several cleavages. For example, some have *cubic* or *rhombohedral* cleavage, which means they split into cubes or rhombohedra. Some minerals, such as pyroxenes and amphiboles, have two cleavages. In any other direction, they break in an irregular way. Irregular breaks are called fractures. Some minerals with no cleavage have a distinctive fracture. For example, obsidian (a rock) and opal (a mineral) have *conchoidal* (shell-like) fracture. Other kinds of fracture include fibrous, hackly (jagged), splintery and earthy.

Above: Azurite is a copper mineral which can be identified by its azure-blue colour. However, colour is not always a good guide to identification. This is because many minerals occur in a variety of colours, which may be caused by impurities.

Streak, the colour of a mineral in powder form, is a guide to the identification of some minerals, because it differs from the normal colour of the mineral. Below: Hematite, an iron mineral, is steel-grey to black in colour. But, if you scrape the surface, the powder you make will be dark red to reddish-brown.

Colour and Streak

One of the most attractive features of minerals is their colour. But colour can be misleading when you are trying to identify a particular specimen, because many minerals occur in a wide variety of colours. The variations may be caused by impurities or by other factors. For example, heat, light, radiation and corrosion can alter the colour of a mineral, and some gemstones are artificially stained by jewellers. Minerals which occur in a variety of colours are called *allochromatic*. But some always have the same colour, although the shade may vary. These minerals are called *idiochromatic*. They include azurite (blue), chalcopyrite (brassy yellow) and malachite (green).

Another test of colour comes when you scrape a mineral and produce a powder. The powder is called the *streak* and it may differ from the colour of the mineral. For example, hematite and magnetite are black iron minerals. But hematite has a reddish-brown streak, while magnetite has a black streak. Streak is, however, of little value in identifying some minerals. For example, most silicates have a white streak.

Iridescence and opalescence cause some minerals to show the colours of the rainbow when they are rotated. These effects result from structural features, such as tiny fissures, within the minerals.

Transparency

When light rays strike a mineral, some are reflected, some are transmitted through the mineral, and some are absorbed. *Transparent* minerals, however thick they may be, transmit light easily and you can see right through them. *Translucent* minerals also transmit some light, but you cannot see through them. *Opaque* minerals do not transmit light to any extent. Instead, they absorb or reflect light rays. These terms are used to describe minerals. Geologists also use the term *subtransparent* for minerals through which objects appear less distinct. Another term, *subtranslucent*, is used for minerals between translucent and opaque ones. But it should be remembered that transparent minerals which are highly coloured or which contain internal flaws may seem to be non-transparent. And non-transparent specimens may become transparent when sliced into extremely thin sections.

Refraction and Dispersion

When light rays pass from air into a mineral, they are bent, or *refracted*. The amount by which they are refracted is called the *refractive index*. The refractive indices of mineral crystals can be measured with complicated scientific instruments. One mineral, cryolite, has the same refractive index as water. As a result, when you place a cryolite crystal in water, it disappears! Jewellers sometimes measure the refractive indices of gems to check whether they are genuine.

Double refraction is a property of some minerals, such as Iceland spar, a pure form of calcite. If a crystal rhombohedron of Iceland spar was put on this page, you would see two images of every word. This happens because each light ray is split in two, and the two parts are refracted at different angles.

When light rays pass through a

Crystal rhombohedra of Iceland spar, a pure form of calcite, have an unusual optical property. They make us see double, as this picture shows.

prism, they are refracted and split into a rainbow-like band of colours called the *spectrum*. This effect, called *dispersion*, is marked in some minerals, especially diamond. Diamond cutters try to obtain the maximum dispersion, to produce the effect which they call *fire*.

Lustre

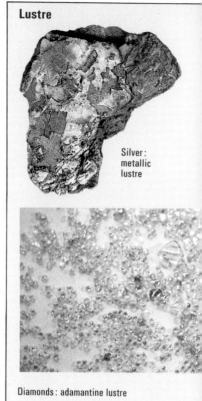

Lustre

Silver: metallic lustre

Diamonds: adamantine lustre

Lustre is another feature of minerals. It describes the surface sheen or gloss. It is determined by the nature of the surface, the extent to which light is reflected and the refractive index. Opaque native elements, such as gold and silver, and most sulphide ores have a shiny metallic lustre. Opaque metallic minerals with a less developed lustre are said to be *submetallic*.

Other lustres are non-metallic. They include *adamantine*, to describe the clear, brilliant lustre of diamond and such minerals as cassiterite, rutile and some zircons. *Vitreous* lustre (like shiny, broken glass) is characteristic of most silicates. *Subvitreous* is a term used for such minerals as calcite, in which the vitreous lustre is less developed. Brown or yellow minerals, resembling amber (page 41), have a *resinous* lustre. *Pearly* lustre occurs when light is reflected from a series of parallel surfaces within the mineral, such as in muscovite. Minerals with fibrous structures have a *silky* lustre. Those with tiny irregularities in their surfaces have a *greasy* lustre. Minerals which lack lustre are said to be *dull* or *earthy*.

Crystals

Most minerals form crystals, but well-developed crystals of many minerals are rare, because the conditions required for them to develop seldom occur in nature.

Crystals form from cooling magma, from vapour emitted around hot springs and volcanoes, and from mineral-rich water. You can see crystals form by a simple experiment. Dissolve alum or salt in water until the water will take no more. Suspend a piece of string in the liquid. As the water evaporates, crystals will form around the string.

Asbestos: pearly lustre

Baryte: vitreous lustre

Opal: resinous to vitreous lustre

Lustre, which is a feature produced by light on the surface of a mineral, is a characteristic of minerals which is often useful in identification. There are various kinds of lustre. Shown here are silver, which has a metallic lustre; asbestos, which has a pearly lustre; baryte, which has a vitreous lustre (like broken glass); diamond, which has an adamantine (brilliant) lustre; and opal, whose lustre varies from resinous (like resin) to vitreous.

The study of crystals is important in identifying minerals, because each mineral has a definite crystal form. This form is related to the arrangement of atoms in the mineral. The science of crystallography is complex. But mineral collectors should know some basic things about crystals.

Crystals display symmetry. Symmetry occurs in many familiar objects, such as boxes, because boxes can be cut in half in such a way that one half is the mirror image of the other. The surface along which the object is cut is called the *plane of symmetry*. Now think of a cube, which is a solid with six square sides (faces). You can cut a cube in nine ways (horizontally, vertically and diagonally) to produce halves which are mirror images of the other halves. This means that a cube has nine planes of symmetry.

Symmetry is also described by axes of symmetry. In the cube, the vertical axis of symmetry is an imaginary line passing through the centre points of the top and bottom faces. Imagine the cube being rotated around this axis. As it rotates, it will present an appearance identical to that at the start four times during one complete revolution. The cube also has two horizontal axes of symmetry, which connect the centre points of the side faces. Hence, a cube has three axes around each of which it can be rotated to give the same orientation four times in one revolution. Crystallographers express this by saying that a cube has 3 four-fold axes of symmetry. The cube also has 6 two-fold axes of symmetry which pass through the edges, and there are 4 three-fold axes passing through the corners. A crystal is said to have a centre of symmetry if, for each face on one side of a crystal, there is another parallel to it on the other side. So a centre of symmetry is present in the cube.

Crystals, however, form in a wide variety of shapes, of which the cube is only one. Each crystal, according to its symmetry, can be classified into one of the seven crystal systems given on page 31. They are defined by the number and types of symmetry elements that are present. To each system are assigned *crystallographic axes* which act as reference lines for the determination of the orientation of each crystal face. In most crystal systems, they lie along axes of symmetry, and they are shown on page 31. The trigonal crystal system has the same set of crystallographic axes as in the hexagonal crystal system. But, while the hexagonal system has one vertical, six-fold axis of symmetry, the trigonal has a three-fold one.

All crystals that belong to the cubic crystal system must each have 4 three-fold axes of symmetry. Galena, garnet and diamond, though they look different, all have the same axes of symmetry. The three crystallographic, or reference, axes, a_1, a_2 and a_3, have the same length and are at right angles to each other.

The tetragonal crystal system is characterized by the presence of one four-fold axis of symmetry. There are three crystallographic axes, with the two horizontal ones, a_1 and a_2, of equal length. But the vertical axis, c, is either longer or shorter.

The orthorhombic crystal system is defined by the presence of 3 two-fold axes of symmetry or one two-fold axis, plus two perpendicular planes of symmetry. The crystallographic axes, a, b and c, are at right angles to each other, but they are all of different lengths.

Crystals of the monoclinic crystal system must contain one two-fold axis of symmetry. The crystallographic axes, a, b and c, are of different lengths. The vertical axis, c, is at right angles to the horizontal axis, b. But axis a is tilted downwards at more than 90°.

Crystals of the triclinic crystal system can have either no symmetry or just a centre of symmetry. The three crystallographic axes, a, b and c, are of different lengths. The angles between the axes (angles $α$, $β$ and $γ$, as shown in the diagram), are not at right angles to each other.

The hexagonal crystal system has one six-fold axis of symmetry, while the trigonal crystal system has one three-fold axis of symmetry. Both systems have the same set of crystallographic axes. The three horizontal ones, a_1, a_2 and a_3, are equal in length and at an angle of 120° to each other. The vertical axis, c, is longer or shorter than the other three axes.

Crystal systems

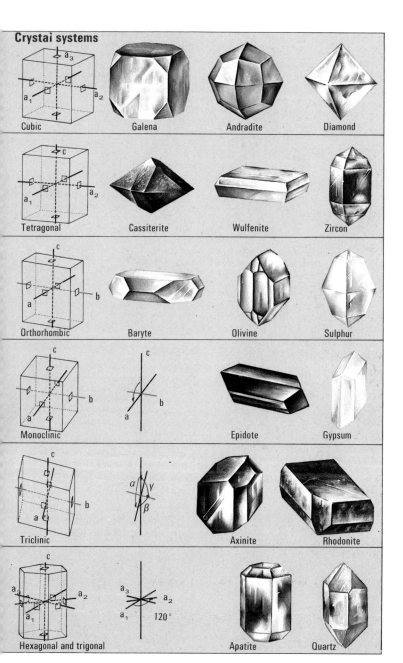

Cubic — Galena — Andradite — Diamond

Tetragonal — Cassiterite — Wulfenite — Zircon

Orthorhombic — Baryte — Olivine — Sulphur

Monoclinic — Epidote — Gypsum

Triclinic — Axinite — Rhodonite

Hexagonal and trigonal — Apatite — Quartz

Rutile crystals

Far left: Crystals of the titanium mineral rutile have the symmetry of the tetragonal system. The crystals are often twinned, left, in a knee- or elbow-shape. On either side of the axis, or 'knee' of the twinned crystal, the forms are identical, being prismatic, and ending in pyramidal shapes.

Twinned Crystals

Crystals do not usually occur singly. Instead, they form in groups in veins, geodes, and so on. Sometimes, crystals develop in contact with each other. Such crystals are called *contact twins*. The picture of rutile on this page is a 'knee-shaped' contact twin. Some crystal twins interpenetrate each other. An example of interpenetrated (or intergrown) crystals occurs in the mineral staurolite (see page 86).

Habit and Aggregates

The crystals of any one mineral all have the same symmetry. But varying conditions, which occur when crystals form, cause the crystals of some minerals to form in a variety of shapes. This may happen when crystals grow more rapidly in one direction than another. For example, quartz crystals always have the symmetry of the trigonal system. But some crystals are long and thin, while others are short and stumpy. Calcite has very varied crystals. Over 80 crystal shapes have been found.

The characteristic shape, or shapes, of mineral crystals are called the *habit*. Geologists use a number of terms to describe habit. For example, *prismatic* habit means

Galena crystals

Gypsum crystal

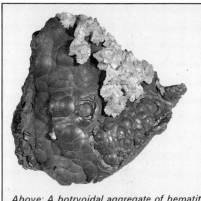

Above: A botryoidal aggregate of hematite.
Right: A dendritic aggregate of copper.

Quartz crystal

Above left: Black crystals of the lead mineral ore, galena, have the symmetry of the cubic system. When struck, the crystals break into even smaller cubes. Left: A crystal of gypsum, a sulphate mineral, of the monoclinic system. Above: An elongated crystal of quartz, has the symmetry of the trigonal system.

that a crystal is much longer in one direction than it is in the other two. Prismatic habit may be *acicular* (needle-like), *bladed* (flattened), *columnar* (column-like), *fibrous* (consisting of long, thin strands) and *stalactitic* (like a stalactite). *Lamellar* habit is the opposite of prismatic, in that the crystals are flattened, such that they are much shorter in one direction than the other two. They may be *tabular* (with broad, flat faces), *foliated* (consisting of layers of thin sheets like mica), and so on.

Many minerals form *aggregates*, which are masses of imperfect crystals. A *massive* aggregate contains small crystal grains which can be seen under a magnifying glass. Massive aggregates with visible grains have a *granular* form. If the grains are so small that they can be seen only through a microscope, the mineral is said to be *cryptocrystalline*. Some aggregates form rounded masses. *Botryoidal* aggregates are like bunches of grapes; *reniform* aggregates are kidney-shaped; and *mamillary* aggregates consist of even larger rounded lumps. Branching aggregates are *dendritic*, while others are moss-like. Other aggregates are *filiform* (thread-like) or wiry. Minerals which crumble easily are *earthy* or *powdery*.

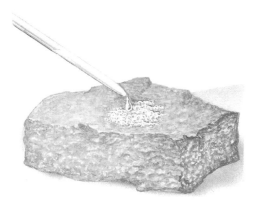

Acid tests are useful in distinguishing between some rocks and minerals. Left: A few drops of hydrochloric acid are placed on limestone. The rock effervesces (fizzes). This effect does not occur when the acid is put on dolomite, a rock which may be confused with limestone.

The Chemistry of Minerals

Apart from the native elements (see page 58), most minerals are combinations of elements. Each element has a symbol, and these symbols are used in the chemical formulae of the minerals. The symbols used in this book are all listed on the opposite page.

Each mineral in the *Guide to Minerals* (pages 58–101) has a chemical formula, which is given after the mineral's name. For example, halite (page 76) has the chemical formula NaCl. From the table, opposite, you will see that Na is the symbol for sodium and Cl represents chlorine. Hence, halite (rock salt) is a chemical combination of equal parts of sodium and chlorine, called sodium chloride.

Other formulae are more complicated. Some contain numbers, such as CaF_2 for fluorite. The figure 2 means that fluorite is a chemical combination, consisting of two atoms of fluorine (F) for every one atom of calcium (Ca). Another point to remember is that you will sometimes see the symbols for two elements, separated by a comma, within a pair of brackets, such as (Mg,Fe). This means that the atoms of magnesium (Mg) and iron (Fe) may substitute for each other. As a result, the formula implies that this is a group, or series, of related minerals, not a single one. For example, olivine has the formula $(Mg,Fe)_2SiO_4$. Olivine is, therefore, the name for a group of minerals which are silicates of magnesium and iron. A magnesium-rich variety of olivine is called forsterite, while an iron-rich variety is fayalite.

Chemical Tests

Analyzing minerals to find their chemical composition is a complicated business. However, there are some simple chemical tests which help us to identify minerals. For example, halite dissolves in water. Two associated minerals, anhydrite and gypsum, are also soluble in water, but they dissolve less readily than halite.

Acid tests are also useful. For example, specimens of wollastonite

Important Chemical Symbols

Ag	Silver	Li	Lithium
Al	Aluminium	Mg	Magnesium
As	Arsenic	Mn	Manganese
Au	Gold	Mo	Molybdenum
B	Boron	Na	Sodium
Ba	Barium	Ni	Nickel
Be	Beryllium	O	Oxygen
Bi	Bismuth	P	Phosphorus
C	Carbon	Pb	Lead
Ca	Calcium	Pt	Platinum
Cl	Chlorine	S	Sulphur
Co	Cobalt	Sb	Antimony
Cr	Chromium	Si	Silicon
Cu	Copper	Sn	Tin
F	Fluorine	Ti	Titanium
Fe	Iron	U	Uranium
H	Hydrogen	V	Vanadium
Hg	Mercury	W	Tungsten
K	Potassium	Zn	Zinc

Above: Flame tests are useful guides to establishing the presence of certain elements in a mineral sample. From left to right: The powder of strontium minerals turns a flame crimson-red; copper minerals turn a flame blue or green; sodium minerals turn a flame yellow; and potassium minerals produce a violet colour.

Lodestone is a kind of magnetite and it has marked magnetic properties. Below: A piece of lodestone attracts iron filings. Below left: Lodestone picks up iron nails.

Left: A photograph of the silicate mineral, willemite, in natural light. Right: In ultraviolet light, the same specimen (from Franklin, New Jersey, USA) fluoresces green. The black areas are franklinite, an ore of zinc.

(page 89) may resemble tremolite (page 90). But wollastonite will dissolve in hydrochloric acid, while tremolite does not react. Some minerals are insoluble in dilute acids, but soluble in concentrated ones. Others react with hot acids and not cold ones. Various helpful acid tests are mentioned in the *Guide to Minerals* section. But acids not only attack minerals. They will also burn skin and clothes, so great care must be taken. Also, you must avoid breathing in acid fumes by using them only in well-aired rooms.

Flame tests help to establish the presence of certain elements in minerals. For these tests, geologists usually use a platinum wire, because platinum is a metal which melts only at a very high temperature. First clean the wire and then pick up a little of the powdered mineral and hold it in a flame. Sodium will burn with a yellow flame, sulphur with a blue flame, calcium with a red flame, barium with a yellowish-green flame, and so on. Hence, you can, for example, test the mineral baryte, an ore of barium, by crushing a small sample and seeing if it turns a flame green.

Other Methods of Identifying Minerals

There are various other tests used to identify minerals which have special and unusual properties. For example, you can confirm your identification of halite by licking it to see if it tastes salty. And the native element, arsenic, and the mineral scorodite both give off a smell resembling garlic when they are heated. A third test involves another of our senses, touch. This applies, for example, to steatite, a variety of the mineral talc, which feels soft and soapy, when we run our fingers over it. However, such tests apply only to a handful of minerals.

Magnetism is a property of only a few minerals, notably magnetite. Some minerals become electrically charged when they are heated or subjected to pressure. For example, if you heat a sample of tourmaline, it will become positively charged at one end and negatively charged at the other. As a result, if you heat a piece of tourmaline in a fire, it will attract the ashes. Quartz is a mineral which is electrically charged by pressure. Artificial quartz crystals are used in electrical equipment, such as some clocks and watches and in radio receivers and transmitters.

Another property of some minerals is luminescence, which means that the minerals glow in shining colours when they are exposed to ultraviolet light or X-rays. This colour may differ from the colour in ordinary light. For example, fluorite fluoresces blue in ultraviolet light and it is from fluorite that the word fluorescence comes. Calcite fluoresces red, pink and yellow; scheelite fluoresces white; and willemite, as shown on page 36, fluoresces green.

An important feature of some minerals is their radioactivity, which can be measured with a Geiger counter. Pitchblende, the massive variety of the mineral, uraninite, is the leading radioactive mineral, because it is the chief ore of uranium, which is used as a fuel in atomic power stations.

Below: A prospector searches for radioactive minerals, particularly the valuable pitchblende (uraninite), the chief ore of uranium, with a Geiger counter. Modern Geiger counters were developed in the 1920s.

Gems and Jewellery

As we have seen, jewellery has been in use since the Stone Age. The reasons for the popularity of jewellery included the love of beautiful things, the desire for personal adornment and the wish to show to others the wearer's wealth or power. Jewellery was also associated with superstitions and magic. All these factors apply, in one way or another, today. For example, in 1969, the actor Richard Burton spent $1·2 million (then about £500,000) for a diamond to adorn his then wife, the actress Elizabeth Taylor. Crown jewels worn by monarchs signify their power and status. And such things as charm bracelets and St Christopher medals (to protect travellers) remind us of ancient beliefs that certain minerals offered protection against evil spirits and illnesses.

Famous Gemstones

Many gemstones have become famous in their own right. For example, the largest diamond ever found was the *Cullinan*, which was named after Sir Thomas Cullinan, chairman of the Premier Mining Company in South Africa. This diamond, measuring about $12\frac{1}{2}$ centimetres (about 5 inches) across, was found at Premier Mine in 1905. It weighed 3106 metric carats. Carats are the units used for weighing gemstones. Five carats equals one gram and, hence, the *Cullinan* weighed 621·2 grams (over $1\frac{1}{3}$ lbs). It was cut into 105 gemstones, the largest of which, called *The Star of Africa No 1*, weighed 516 carats. This stone is still the world's largest cut diamond. It now adorns the British Royal Sceptre (see page 15). The second largest stone cut from the *Cullinan* is in the British Imperial State Crown (shown opposite). This superb diamond weighs 309 carats.

Other famous diamonds include the Indian *Koh-i-noor* (Persian for *Mountain of Light*), which was presented to Queen Victoria in 1850. The history of this diamond has been traced back to 1304. It changed hands several times as a result of war and conquest. Another famous

Left: Jade belt ornaments made in China between the 1200s and 1700s. Jade ornaments are made from two minerals: jadeite (see page 89) and nephrite (page 91).

The British Imperial State Crown contains over 3000 jewels, including a large diamond and the Black Prince's ruby (which is really a spinel, see page 74).

Pearls are used in jewellery, but they are not minerals, because they are of organic origin. The best pearls come from sea pearl oysters, which live in warm seas. Pearls are composed of nacre, a substance made by the oysters. The nacre accumulates in layers around specks of foreign matter, such as grains of sand.

gemstone is the *Orloff* diamond, which was once part of the Russian crown jewels. It was bought, in Amsterdam, by Count Orloff who gave it to Catherine the Great, Empress of Russia, in an unsuccessful attempt to win back her favour. This diamond was supposed to have been the eye of an Indian idol, which stood in a Brahmin temple.

Materials used in Jewellery

Gold, silver and platinum are valuable metals used in jewellery. Gold is especially important, because it is easy to work and it does not tarnish, as silver does. The leading gemstones are diamonds, especially colourless ones, and three coloured gems, rubies and sapphires (varieties of the mineral corundum), and emeralds (varieties of beryl). Probably the most valuable of these gems is now the ruby. These four gemstones have several features in common. They are all hard and, hence, long-wearing. Their hardness ranges from diamond, the hardest of all natural substances, to ruby and sapphire, which rate 9 on the Mohs' scale, and emerald, which has a hardness of 8. They are also all transparent and sparkle magnificently after they have been cut and polished. Fine gemstone varieties of these minerals are rare, which adds to their value.

The annual world production of diamonds in the mid-1970s was about 46 million carats (about 9200 kg, or just over 9 tons). But less than one-fourth of the diamonds produced are suitable for jewellery. The rest are used in industry. Leading producers of diamonds are Zaire, the USSR and South Africa. Major producers of rubies and sapphires are Burma, Sri Lanka (Ceylon) and Thailand. The most superb emeralds come from Colombia, in South America.

Many other minerals are used in jewellery. They include transparent varieties of garnets, peridot, various types of quartz, sphene, spinel, spodumene, topaz, tourmaline, turquoise and zircon. Jewellers also use translucent but beautifully-coloured minerals, including agate, chalcedony and jadeite. Some minerals are prized, because they contain interesting fibrous structures. For example, some chrysoberyls and specimens of tiger's eye (page 95) display a cat's eye effect, called *chatoyancy*, when they are rotated. Some rubies and sapphires display *asterism*, caused by internal fibres arranged like stars. And some opals are extremely popular because they show a play of colours, called *opalescence*. All the gemstones mentioned here are described in the *Guide to Minerals* section of this book.

Some other substances used in jewellery include amber, coral, ivory, jet (a kind of coal, page 119), pearls and tortoiseshell. None of these, however, is a mineral. They are all of organic origin.

Cutting Gemstones
In order to show off the best qualities of a gemstone, it must be cut and polished. The best minerals for jewellery are hard, and so special

Amber is not a mineral. It is the hardened resin from pine trees. Amber sometimes contains the fossilized remains of insects which were trapped in the sticky resin millions of years ago.

Above: These uncut rubies are rare gemstone varieties of the mineral corundum (see page 75). Left: At the Gibson ruby mine in North Carolina, in the United States, workers sift through loose rocks and extract any rubies they may find. The rubies are later cut and polished and used in jewellery.

materials must be used to cut and polish them. In the case of rubies and sapphires, carborundum, an artificial silicon carbide, can be used. But the only material which can cut and polish diamond is diamond itself.

The chief aims of a lapidary (or gem-cutter) are to remove all flaws, make the best use of the mineral's optical qualities, waste as little of the specimen as possible, and, in the case of coloured minerals, to achieve the best colour. To get the best optical qualities from a transparent gemstone, the lapidary must cut a series of facets (inclined surfaces) on the top and bottom of the stone. If the facets are the right size and shape, and cut at the correct angles to each other, they will reflect light back out of the gemstone. Particularly in the case of the diamond, the facets also disperse light, producing a play of colours, called fire.

Skilled lapidaries use several methods of cutting, some of which were specially developed for particular gemstones. For example, the brilliant cut was invented, in the 1700s, for the diamond. This cut usually has 58 facets, although some varieties have more. Diagrams showing the top (crown), side (girdle) and the bottom (pavilion) of the brilliant cut are shown on page 44. Variations of the brilliant cut are the boat-shaped *navette* or *marquise*, and the pear-shaped *pendoloque*. Brilliant cuts are also used for other gemstones, including the green demantoid garnet and zircons.

The step, or trap, cut has parallel facets cut across the top and bottom. It is also called the emerald cut, because it is often used for that gemstone, as well as aquamarines, tourmalines, and so on. Sometimes, gemstones, such as sapphires, are given a brilliant top but a step cut bottom. This is called a mixed cut.

Another cut used for small diamonds, pyropes (ruby-red garnets) and other stones is called the rose cut. This has a flat bottom, but the top has 12 or 24 facets which end in a central point, giving the stone a shape like a hemisphere. Among other cuts, the cabochon is important. It consists essentially of a circular or elliptical stone with a domed surface. It is used for a wide variety of gemstones, and is particularly suitable for opaque minerals and those that contain fibrous structures, such as tiger's eye (page 95).

Home-made Jewellery

Many mineral collectors like to polish their specimens to make them as attractive as possible. This is only one step away from making your own jewellery and ornaments.

Polishing minerals by hand is a slow and laborious job. But it is now possible to buy equipment which does the work for you. The basic item is a tumbler. This consists of a rotating drum, operated by an electric motor. You place pebbles or mineral chips in a drum, together

Right: A craftsman carefully cleans a diamond, which is the hardest of all natural substances. Uncut diamonds are often dull-looking and sometimes covered by a greyish film. Cleaning, cutting and polishing turn them into brilliant gemstones.

Below: This diamond necklace, designed by Wendy Ramshaw, won an international award in 1975.

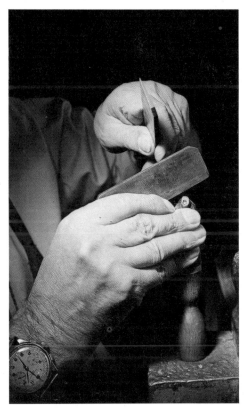

with grinding and polishing agents, and water. As the drum rotates, the specimens are ground and polished. This action reproduces what happens on a beach when wave action grinds pebbles against each other, but it speeds up the process. It also exposes the true colour of the specimens by stripping away outer, weathered layers. To find out about the various kinds of tumblers and how much they cost, enquire at a shop selling minerals and rocks, join a lapidary club, or get a magazine for amateurs, which advertises them. There are other instruments you can get if you want to do more elaborate work. For example, you can buy slabbing saws to slice through minerals, lapping wheels for polishing flat surfaces and instruments for faceting specimens.

Polished minerals can be used to make all kinds of things. They can be stuck on the sides of vases, ash trays and similar objects. They can also be mounted on rings, bracelets, key rings and cufflinks. All you need is a powerful adhesive, such as epoxy resin. In some parts of the world, it is possible, though unlikely, that you will find diamond, ruby, sapphire or even nuggets of gold in river or beach pebbles. But specimens of varieties of quartz, agate and chalcedony are much more common. Even some rocks take a high polish and can be very attractive. The best

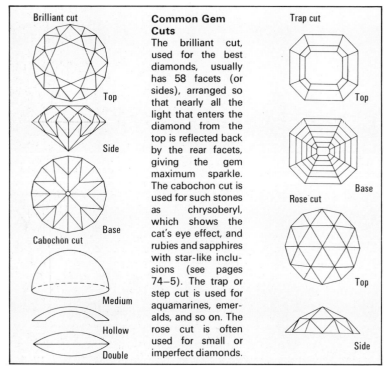

Common Gem Cuts

The brilliant cut, used for the best diamonds, usually has 58 facets (or sides), arranged so that nearly all the light that enters the diamond from the top is reflected back by the rear facets, giving the gem maximum sparkle. The cabochon cut is used for such stones as chrysoberyl, which shows the cat's eye effect, and rubies and sapphires with star-like inclusions (see pages 74–5). The trap or step cut is used for aquamarines, emeralds, and so on. The rose cut is often used for small or imperfect diamonds.

specimens are smooth-textured and hard, so that they will wear well. Coarse-grained, porous or pitted specimens should be avoided.

Synthetic and Imitation Gemstones

The demand for gemstones for jewellery and also for industry has led to the development of techniques to produce synthetic stones. The most important is the production of rubies and sapphires by the flame fusion process, which involves melting pure alumina powder in oxygen and hydrogen (see diagram below). Synthetic rubies are used in lasers, but these artificial stones have not affected the price or demand for real stones. Many synthetic stones contain minute air bubbles or specks of unfused powder. Other gemstones which are made artificially include emerald, rutile and spinel. Synthetic diamonds have been made since 1955. But they are small and not of gem quality. Their cost is also high, considering that they can be used only for making abrasives and polishing powders.

Imitation stones are made essentially from a mixture of silicates, which form a soft glass, or *paste*. These stones are easily scratched. Plastic imitations are also manufactured.

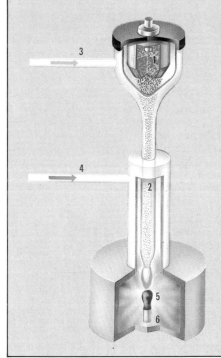

Synthetic Gems

One way of making cheap but good-quality rubies and sapphires (forms of aluminium oxide, or corundum) is shown here. The process is called the flame-fusion or Verneuil method, after its inventor. Pure alumina powder (1) is released into a central chamber (2), while oxygen enters through a tube (3). Another gas, hydrogen, enters from the tube (4) to feed an oxyhydrogen flame in the chamber. The high temperature fuses the powder into droplets, which develop into a cylindrical boule, or gem (5), on a fire clay support (6). The diameter of the boule is controlled by lowering the fire clay support and varying the flow of the gases. Many synthetic rubies, sapphires and spinels are made in this way, but real stones have kept their value.

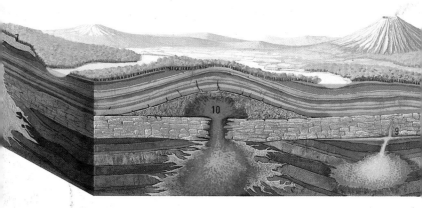

The Formation of Rocks

Geologists divide rocks into three main groups, according to the ways in which they were formed. The three groups are igneous rocks, sedimentary rocks and metamorphic rocks.

Igneous Rocks

Igneous rocks are formed from magma, which has cooled and hardened. Magma may flow from volcanoes or from long fissures (openings in the ground) as lava. When lava solidifies, it forms such rocks as basalt (page 106) and andesite (page 107).

Magma may, when it reaches the surface, be formed into pyroclastic (fragmented) rocks. Pyroclasts are fragments of lava ejected into the air during volcanic eruptions. They range in size from fine volcanic dust and ash to lapilli (small stones) and volcanic bombs. Some bombs are about the size of a loaf. Others, weighing more than 100 tonnes, may be hurled long distances during violent eruptions. Examples of pyroclastic rocks are shown on pages 108–9. All rocks which form from magma on the Earth's surface are called *extrusive* igneous rocks.

Often, however, magma cools and solidifies underground into *intrusive* igneous rocks. But intrusive rocks may be exposed at the surface millions of years after they were formed. This is because the overlying rocks have been worn away, or removed by tectonic processes.

ground to create intrusive igneous rocks. Steeply-inclined sheets of magma form dykes (8). Sills (9) are parallel to existing beds. Some bodies called laccoliths (10) push up the overlying rocks into domes. The largest masses of magma are batholiths (not shown here).

Left: A fountain of molten lava shoots upwards from the vent of Kilauea Iki volcano in November, 1959. Kilauea Iki is on Hawaii, the largest of a group of volcanic islands in the North Pacific Ocean. The islands are the tips of volcanoes which have risen from the ocean bed. More than half of the volcanoes are hidden beneath the waves.

47

The Giant's Causeway, in Northern Ireland, is composed of basalt, an extrusive igneous rock. When basaltic lava cools, it sometimes splits and shrinks into hexagonal columns, which resemble giant stepping stones.

Intrusive igneous rocks occur in a variety of shapes and sizes. For example, enormous dome-shaped masses, called *batholiths*, often underlie mountain chains. They are often composed of granite, the commonest intrusive igneous rock (see pages 102–3). Smaller formations also occur. *Dykes* are steeply-inclined sheets of solidified magma, while *ring dykes* are circular outcrops, which are sometimes intruded around an existing block of rock. *Sills* are sheets of igneous rock which are parallel to beds of existing rocks. They are often horizontal. *Laccoliths* also spread horizontally, but they are similar to batholiths in that they often push up overlying rocks into domes. Intrusive rocks may be *abyssal* or *plutonic* (formed at great depths) or *hypabyssal* (formed near the surface). (See pages 102–5.)

Textures of Igneous Rocks

Geologists have several ways of classifying and studying igneous rocks. The size of the grains is important. When magma cools slowly, there is time for sizeable crystals (or grains) to form, and so rocks formed by slow cooling are mostly medium or coarse-grained. Medium and coarse-grained rocks are mostly intrusive. Most of the grains in coarse-grained rocks are more than 1–2 millimetres (0·04–0·08 inches) across. Medium-grained rocks have grains which are between 1–2 millimetres and 0·1 millimetres (0·004 inches) across. The grains in fine-grained rocks are less than 0·1 millimetres across. Fine-grained igneous rocks are usually extrusive, because the rapid cooling on the surface leaves no time for sizeable crystals to form. Some extrusive igneous rocks have cooled so quickly that they solidify into volcanic glass, like the rock obsidian (see page 108).

Rocks in which the grains are all about the same size are said to have a *granular texture*. However, the temperatures at which minerals crystallize vary. Hence, some minerals crystallize into sizeable grains while the rest of the magma is still molten. But, if the cooling then speeds up, other minerals may crystallize into tiny grains. Rocks with large grains (called *phenocrysts*) set in a fine-grained *groundmass* are said to have a *porphyritic* texture. *Fluidal* or *flow* texture describes rocks in which the grains have been aligned with their lengths parallel to the direction of the flow of the magma.

Structures of Igneous Rocks

Other important features relate to the structure of igneous rocks. Some have a *vesicular* structure, because they contain vesicles (holes) formed by gas. Vesicles which are filled, at a later stage, by other minerals are called *amygdales*, and the rock structure is *amygdaloidal*. Some igneous rocks contain fragments of other rocks, called *xenoliths*. Igneous rocks may also be *banded* or *layered*, the layers being composed of different minerals. Furthermore, when magma cools, it may shrink and break, forming joints (vertical cracks). For example, basalt may break into hexagonal columns. Chemically, there are four main kinds of igneous rocks: acid, intermediate, basic and ultrabasic. For an explanation of these terms, see page 102.

Two intrusive igneous rocks. Left: Hay Tor, Dartmoor, England, is a tough granite outcrop. Below: A dyke exposed at the surface.

Natural forces steadily wear away the land. Above: The Italian Dolomites are steep mountains. But frost action shatters the rock and loose fragments tumble downhill and accumulate in piles called talus or scree at the foot of the slope. Below left: The Aletsch glacier, in Switzerland, is a moving body of ice. It wears away the land and carries worn material, called moraine, downhill. Below right: The Hapicuru River, in Brazil, sweeps worn fragments of rock into the Atlantic Ocean, discolouring the water. Opposite: In deserts, the wind blows sand across the land, acting like a natural sandblaster, undercutting exposed rocks.

Sedimentary Rocks

Sedimentary rocks are of three main kinds. *Clastic* sedimentary rocks are formed from fragments of rock worn from the land. *Chemical* sedimentary rocks are formed by chemical action. This occurs, for example, when water containing dissolved minerals evaporates and some of the minerals are precipitated (released) from the water to form solid rock. The third type is *organic* sedimentary rock. This is composed mostly of the remains of parts of once-living organisms. Sedimentary rocks cover about 75 per cent of the world's land areas. But they form only 5 per cent of all the rocks in the top 16 km (10 miles) of the Earth's crust. The rest are igneous or metamorphic rocks.

Clastic Sedimentary Rocks

The Earth's surface is always changing. Freezing water in cool, moist regions and rapid changes of temperature in hot deserts split and shatter rocks. Such processes are called *mechanical weathering*. Also, *chemical weathering* dissolves and decomposes some rocks. This may occur, for example, when rainwater reacts chemically with rocks. This happens because rainwater usually dissolves some carbon dioxide from the air and so it becomes a weak acid.

Other tremendous natural forces are also at work. They include running water, such as rivers, moving bodies of ice (glaciers and ice sheets) and the wind, particularly in dry regions. These forces erode (wear away) the land. They also transport loose fragments of rock. As the bits of rock are moved along, they rub against each other. In this way, they are rounded and ground down into smaller and smaller pieces. Finally, the worn material comes to rest, usually in water and sometimes on land. There, the sediment, as it is then called, becomes compacted and cemented to form hard sedimentary rocks. Natural cements are minerals which are precipitated from water which seeps through the grains. Such cementing minerals include anhydrite, calcite, dolomite, iron oxides, pyrite and silica.

Clastic rocks are classified according to the size of their grains. The three main types are coarse-grained *rudaceous* rocks; medium-grained *arenaceous* rocks; and fine-grained *argillaceous* rocks.

Particles in rudaceous rocks are usually more than 2 millimetres (0·08 inches) across, but those with grains larger than 25·4 centimetres (10 inches) across are often called boulder beds. Rudaceous rocks include conglomerates and breccias. In conglomerates, the large fragments are rounded pebbles cemented in fine material (the *matrix*). The pebbles were smoothed during transportation. Breccias contain jagged, angular fragments, which have not been moved far.

Arenaceous rocks contain grains between $\frac{1}{16}$ and 2 mm (0·002–0·08 inches) across. Typical rocks of this kind are sandstones.

Argillaceous rocks are composed of grains which are mostly between $\frac{1}{256}$ and $\frac{1}{16}$ mm (0·0002–0·002 inches) across. They include siltstones. Some mudstones and shales consist of even finer grains.

Above: Around these hot springs in Turkey, the mineral-rich water precipitates calcite, as travertine. This has created a series of terraces. Right: A section through limestone shows how it is riddled with caves and tunnels, dissolved out by rainwater containing carbon dioxide, which makes it a weak acid. Some of the dissolved calcite is re-deposited in the caves by precipitation, caused when dripping water evaporates. Beautiful deposits include stalactites (1), stalagmites (2) and natural columns (3). Streams enter caves from the surface (4) and re-emerge near the base of the limestone (5).

Chemical Sedimentary Rocks

Several chemical sedimentary rocks, called *evaporites*, are formed from seawater. On average, in every 1000 parts of seawater, there are 35 parts of dissolved material. Many elements are present in seawater, but the chief ones are chlorine and sodium, which together form sodium chloride or rock salt (halite). Hence, when seawater evaporates, large deposits of white halite are left behind. Other evaporites include potassium and magnesium salts, gypsum or anhydrite.

Limestone is a rock which may be chemical, clastic (composed of fragments of pre-existing limestones) or organic in origin. One chemical limestone is composed of great numbers of tiny spheres, called ooliths. Ooliths consist of layer upon layer of calcite, deposited around a core, such as a grain of sand or a bit of shell. Another form of chemical limestone occurs in stalactites and stalagmites in limestone caves. These and other beautiful deposits are precipitated from water highly charged with calcite. Calcite deposits, called travertine (see page 116), also form around hot springs.

Other chemical sedimentary rocks include sedimentary iron ores, which are deposited by iron-rich water, and some cherts and flints, which are lumps of silica deposited in cavities in rocks. Bauxite is another chemically-formed rock, created by chemical weathering in hot, wet climates (see page 63).

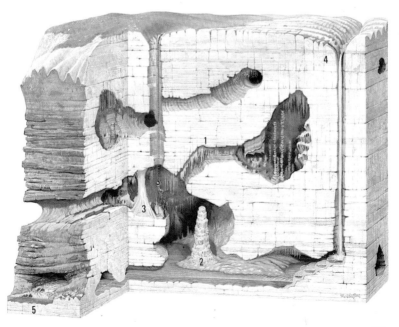

One of the simplest ways of recognizing clastic sedimentary rocks is that they are mostly layered, or stratified. The distinctive bedding planes are formed as layer upon layer of material is deposited. These bedded sandstones are in Zion National Park, in Utah, in the USA.

Organic Sedimentary Rocks

Most sedimentary rocks contain very little organic matter. But some consist mostly of parts of once-living organisms. For example, some limestones are composed of coral, animal shells, or the remains of tiny plants and animals, such as algae or foraminiferids. Some of these limestones form on deep-sea beds, where they accumulate slowly. Other organic rocks are called bone beds. These usually thin layers consist of fossil bones, scales, teeth and so on. Some cherts are rich in the remains of tiny sea animals called radiolarians, and some phosphatic deposits are accumulations of the excreta of sea birds or bats. Coal is an organic rock formed from land plants and you can see the first stage in coal formation in peat bogs. The coal we burn was produced by the drying and alteration of peaty deposits. Types of coal are described on pages 118–9.

Below: In the Carboniferous period, more than 280 million years ago, swampy forests spread over large areas. When the plants died, the rotting material was buried and compressed into coal, an organic sedimentary rock.

Features of Sedimentary Rocks

Sedimentary rocks have been extremely important in helping scientists to unravel the story of life on Earth. This is because many sedimentary rocks contain fossils, the remains or simply evidence of once-living animals and plants. Fossils are also useful guides to dating rocks. Some animal species lived only a comparatively short time before they became extinct. Hence, when their fossils occur in rocks, even though they may be large distances apart, we know that those rocks were formed at about the same time in Earth history.

Many fossils are found in the bedding planes in sedimentary rocks. Bedding planes are seen as distinct lines in sections of exposed sedimentary rocks. They represent the divisions between one rock layer and another. Rock layers, or *strata*, may be several metres thick. Some, called *laminae*, are less than 1 centimetre (0·4 inches) thick. When the strata were formed, they were mostly horizontal, having accumulated on level or gently-sloping floors of seas and lakes. But many sedimentary rocks are now tilted or folded, the result of Earth movements. Generally, in sedimentary rocks, younger rocks overlie older rocks. Often, you will find that one layer overlies another which is many millions of years older. This gap in the time sequence is called an *unconformity*. It may have been caused by the erosion of great thicknesses of rock which once covered the older layer. After the long period of erosion, new sediments again began to accumulate on the old, exposed layer.

Below: Sea animals, called coral polyps, secrete calcite to form cup-like external skeletons. These skeletons form a kind of limestone. Fossils occur in sedimentary rocks. Right: The shoulder blade of a dinosaur is exposed in rocks in the Dinosaur National Monument, in Utah in the USA.

Metamorphic Rocks

Metamorphic rocks result from the alteration of igneous or sedimentary rocks through the action of pressure, heat or chemically active fluids (metasomatism). *Dynamic metamorphism* is caused by pressure alone. *Contact metamorphism* is caused by heat given out by magma. Heat bakes and changes rocks, much as dough is changed into bread when it is baked in an oven. Around a large intrusion of magma, there may be a contact metamorphic *aureole*, or zone, some 2–3 km (1–2 miles) thick. *Regional metamorphism* is caused by pressure and heat. It occurs in areas where mountains are being formed, and its effects may extend for several hundred kilometres.

Minerals may crystallize and become re-arranged in layers or bands during metamorphism. Also, new minerals which were not present in the original rock may be formed. Such minerals include garnet, andalusite, sillimanite and kyanite (pages 84–5), and staurolite and cordierite (pages 86–7). Metamorphic rocks can be grouped according to their textures. *Slaty rocks* are fine-grained and split into thin sheets. *Schistose rocks* also have good cleavage, but they are coarser. *Granular rocks*, such as marble and quartzite, have no cleavage. And *gneisses* are characterized by coarse grains and irregular banding. Examples of metamorphic rocks are shown on pages 120–1.

Below: The diagram shows how pressure and heat during mountain building metamorphoses the sedimentary rock shale into slate. And heat from magma transforms limestones into the metamorphic rock, marble.

Opposite: The Carrara marble quarry in Italy produces superb marble for sculpture. The marble was often used by the great sculptor Michelangelo, whose 'Pietà', in St Peter's Basilica, in Vatican City, Rome, is inset.

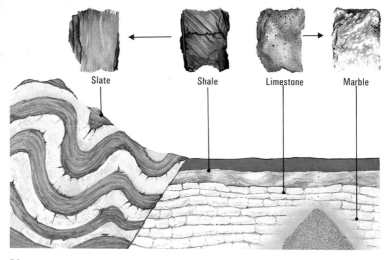

Slate   Shale   Limestone   Marble

Guide to Minerals

The minerals in this Guide are grouped mainly according to their chemical composition. Most minerals are combinations of several chemical elements. But native elements, the first to be described in this Guide, are pure or nearly pure elements. They have not been combined with other elements, such as oxygen or sulphur.

Native elements include several metals, but the chief sources of most metals used in everyday life are mineral ores. The important ores described on pages 63–73, are combinations of elements. Although there are some exceptions, the chief metal ores are sulphides (combinations of a metal with sulphur), and oxides (combinations of a metal with oxygen). The chemical formulae of sulphides contain S, S_2, and so on. The formulae of oxides contain O, O_2, and so on. For example, the mineral magnetite (page 64), a major iron ore, is iron oxide. Its chemical formula is Fe_3O_4. (The chemical formula of each element and mineral follows its name.)

The rest of the Guide (pages 74–101) contains examples of minerals belonging to other chemical groups (including some oxides which are not mineral ores on pages 74–5).

Native elements

Native or *free* elements are rare and only 22 occur naturally. But some native elements occur in more than one form. For example, carbon occurs both as the prized diamond and the more humble, but also useful graphite.

Gold Au

This soft but heavy yellow metal has been a symbol of power and wealth since ancient times, because of its rarity and its special properties. Gold objects date back to the early Stone Age. Gold was once used for coins, but most of the world's gold is now stored in closely guarded bank vaults. But gold has many uses in jewellery, medicine, dentistry and industry – for

Gold nugget

Silver (Mexico)

Silver

plating and making scientific and electrical apparatus.

Native gold occurs most often as grains, dendritic (branching) growths and, sometimes, as rounded nuggets. The rare crystals belong to the cubic system. Gold has no cleavage, and it is easy to work and shape. It resists chemical attack. It does not tarnish in air and does not dissolve in acids, apart from *aqua regia*, a mixture of concentrated nitric and hydrochloric acids. Pure gold has a specific gravity of $19 \cdot 3$ and a hardness of $2\frac{1}{2}$–3. The colour ranges from shining gold-yellow to pale yellow, if it contains much silver. This opaque metal may be confused with pyrite (see page 24) or chalcopyrite (page 68).

Gold occurs in hydrothermal veins, where it crystallized from hot solutions. It is often found in association with quartz (as in the picture on page 58) or with sulphide minerals, especially pyrite. As the surrounding rocks are weathered, the resistant gold is exposed and washed into streams. It may often then become concentrated in alluvial deposits.

Copper

Silver Ag

This beautiful, rare and precious metal has been used in jewellery since ancient times and silver beads made in ancient Egypt date back 6000 years or so. Silver is a fairly unreactive metal, although it dissolves in nitric acid and tarnishes in air polluted by sulphur. It is used for plating and in the electronics and photographic industries. It was once made into coins, but cupro-nickel (an alloy of copper and nickel) is now often used instead. Silver often occurs as scaly, branching or wiry forms. The pure metal belongs to the cubic crystal system.

The specific gravity of pure silver is $10 \cdot 5$ and the hardness is $2\frac{1}{2}$–3. It has no cleavage and it is easy to work and shape. The colour and streak of this opaque metal are silver-white, but it tarnishes to grey or black.

Silver, like gold, often occurs in hydrothermal veins. It often contains some gold or mercury.

Copper Cu

Copper is one of the more widely distributed native elements. It is not very reactive, but it tarnishes in the air and dissolves in nitric acid. Copper was probably the first metal used to make ornaments, tools and weapons, some 10,000 years ago. Around 3000 BC, it was used with tin to make the alloy bronze. Later, it was used with zinc to make brass. Today it has many uses, especially in the electrical industry, because it is the best low-cost conductor of electricity.

Copper crystals have the symmetry of the cubic system. The native element often has a dendritic (branching) shape. The specific gravity is $8 \cdot 9$ and the hardness is $2\frac{1}{2}$–3. It has no cleavage and is extremely ductile, that is, it can be drawn into threads. This opaque metal is copper-red and the streak is pale red, but it tarnishes to dark brown and the surface is often coated with blue (azurite) or green (malachite) crusts. It occurs in hydrothermal veins in lavas, sandstones and conglomerates. The Latin name *cuprum* comes from Cyprium (Cyprus), where the Romans mined it.

Platinum Pt

This rare and precious metal resembles silver. Its name comes from the Spanish word *platina*, a diminutive form of *plata*, Spanish for silver. Platinum melts at 1772°C (3222°F), while silver melts at 962°C (1764°F). Platinum is also less reactive than silver. It resists corrosion and does not tarnish in the air. Like gold, it dissolves only in hot *aqua regia*. Because of this resistance, it is used in equipment for chemical laboratories, as well as in jewellery.

Distorted crystals of platinum, belonging to the cubic system, may occur, but, more often, platinum is found as irregular grains, scales or nuggets. The specific gravity of pure platinum is 21·5. In nature, it always contains some iron and often some copper, giving it a lower specific gravity of 14—19. The hardness is 4—4½ and it is easily shaped. This opaque metal is steel-grey to silver-white. It occurs in igneous rocks, often in association with chromite, and in nickel-bearing rocks.

Iron Fe

Iron forms five per cent of the elements in the Earth's crust, but it rarely occurs as a native element, because it combines so readily with other elements. The iron which is so important in industry comes from various iron ores. The chief iron ores are described on pages 64—5 of this book. Nickel-iron alloy (Ni-Fe) is found in meteorites (see pages 122—3).

Native iron occurs mostly as grains or masses, commonly where volcanic rocks have cut through coal seams. The rare crystals belong to the cubic system. The specific gravity is about 7·5 and the hardness is 4½. The colour of this opaque metal is steel-grey to black. An important feature is its strongly magnetic character.

Arsenic As

Arsenic is an extremely poisonous element, used to make rat poisons, weed killers and insecticides. This metal occurs only fairly rarely as a native element. Well-formed crystals are rare. They show that arsenic belongs to the trigonal crystal system and they have perfect cleavage parallel to the base. Arsenic is usually found in granular, botryoidal (grape-like), or stalactite-like forms. The specific gravity is 5·6—5·8 and the hardness is 3½. The colour is light grey, but it darkens as the surface tarnishes. When heated, arsenic may give off poisonous white fumes which smell like garlic. Arsenic occurs in hydrothermal veins

Platinum nugget found in an alluvial deposit

Arsenic

in both igneous and metamorphic rocks. It is associated with cobalt, nickel and silver ores.

Bismuth Bi

Bismuth is a metal used in medicines, pigments, and alloys that melt easily, such as solders and fuses. This is because bismuth melts at 270°C (518°F). Crystalline bismuth belongs to the trigonal system but well-formed crystals are rare. Bismuth occurs mostly in granular or tree- and moss-like forms. It has perfect basal cleavage. The specific gravity is 9·7–9·8 and the hardness is 2–2½. This silver-white element tarnishes to a reddish colour. It dissolves in nitric acid. Bismuth is found in hydrothermal veins, often in association with ores of cobalt, nickel, silver and tin.

Antimony Sb

Antimony, another poisonous element, is used in alloys for making such things as pewter and it is also used in the manufacture of pigments used for paints and dyes. Women in ancient Egypt and Asia once used compounds of antimony to paint their eyebrows and eyelashes.

Antimony belongs to the trigonal crystal system, but well-formed crystals are rare. They have perfect basal cleavage. Usually, when antimony occurs as a native element, it is as massive or kidney-shaped forms. The specific gravity is 6·6–6·7 and the hardness is 3–3½. This opaque, light grey metal occurs in hydrothermal veins. It is often associated with ores of antimony, arsenic and silver.

Graphite C

Also called plumbago or black lead, graphite is pure carbon. But only a small proportion of graphite which is mined is used in pencils. Far more is used in electrodes, nuclear reactors, fire-resistant crucibles and in steel-making. It is also an important lubricant. Graphite quite commonly occurs as layered masses and may be earthy in appearance. It belongs to the hexagonal system and has a perfect cleavage parallel to the base. The specific gravity is 2·1–2·3 and the hardness is 1–2. This opaque, black to steel-grey mineral marks paper and is greasy to the touch. It is similar in appearance to molybdenite (see page 70). Graphite is a fairly common native element. Flakes of graphite occur in metamorphic rocks, and in veins in igneous rocks. Graphite has the same chemical composition as diamond, but the minerals differ great-

Bismuth in quartz (Connecticut, USA)

Antimony

Graphite (New York, USA)

ly, because the atoms in graphite are in a different structural arrangement from those in diamond. This phenomenon is called polymorphism. It also occurs in other minerals (see page 85).

Diamond C

Like graphite, diamond is pure carbon. But, unlike graphite, diamond was formed under great pressure in pipe-like rock structures of kimberlite (a rare kind of peridotite), which originated in the upper mantle. Diamond is the hardest of all natural substances. Its hardness (10) makes it an excellent abrasive, while its effect on light makes it a prized gemstone, especially after skilled cutting and polishing.

Crystals of diamond belong to the cubic system (see diagram, page 31). Diamond has perfect octahedral cleavage, so that it can be split into an eight-faced double pyramid. But diamond is also brittle and has a conchoidal (shell-like) fracture. The most prized diamonds are colourless, but green, brown, yellow, pink and black diamonds occur. The specific gravity is 3·5. Diamond is mined from kimberlite and alluvial deposits.

Diamonds, cut and polished

Sulphur S

This soft, bright yellow, or sometimes brownish native element is important in the chemical industry. It is used to make sulphuric acid, matches, insecticides, gunpowder, and so on.

The transparent to translucent crystals have the symmetry of the orthorhombic system. They have poor cleavage and fracture unevenly. Sulphur also occurs in crusty masses. The specific gravity is 2–2·1 and the hardness is $1\frac{1}{2}$–$2\frac{1}{2}$. The streak is white and the lustre is resinous to greasy. Sulphur burns with a pale blue flame, giving off acrid fumes. It does not dissolve in water. The melting point is 113°C (235°F). Sulphur occurs around volcanic vents and in some sedimentary rocks, often in association with calcite and gypsum.

Sulphur

Mineral Ores
Pages 63–73 of this Guide are devoted to important mineral ores.

Bauxite
Bauxite is the only important source of aluminium, an important metal in the modern world. But bauxite is not a mineral. It contains several minerals, notably boehmite, diaspore and gibbsite. Bauxite may be earthy or it may consist of granular masses. Its colour may be red, yellow, brown or grey. Bauxite forms in the tropics, where weathering and leaching (the removal of minerals from surface layers by rain and water in the soil) act on rocks containing aluminium silicates. The silicates are removed, and hydrous aluminium oxides are left behind. *Hydrous* means that water is chemically combined in the minerals.

Bauxite (Sierra Leone)

Boehmite AlO(OH)
Boehmite has a dull, earthy lustre. The crystals, belonging to the orthorhombic system, are tiny. They have one good cleavage. The specific gravity is 3–3·1 and the hardness is 3. The colour is white.

Diaspore

Diaspore AlO(OH)
Diaspore is often associated with corundum in emery deposits. It also occurs in limestones and chlorite schists. This transparent to translucent mineral belongs to the orthorhombic crystal system. The crystals have one perfect cleavage. The specific gravity is 3·3–3·5 and the hardness is $6\frac{1}{2}$–7. The colour varies from white or grey to brown or pink.

Gibbsite Al(OH)$_3$
The crystals of gibbsite belong to the monoclinic system. This transparent to translucent mineral occurs in hydrothermal veins. It is mostly white, but may be green, pink or red. The specific gravity is 2·4 and the hardness $2\frac{1}{2}$–$3\frac{1}{2}$. It has perfect basal cleavage. The streak is white.

Gibbsite (stalagmitic habit)
Massachusetts, USA

Iron ores

Hematite

Magnetite

Iron Ores

Iron, a common and tough metal, occurs only rarely as a native element (see page 60). Iron is, therefore, extracted from ores. Two of the most important are oxides, magnetite and hematite. Goethite, another oxide, is a less important ore, but it is an attractive mineral. A fourth, important source of iron, siderite, is a carbonate.

Magnetite Fe_3O_4

One of the characteristic properties of magnetite is that it is strongly magnetic and so grains can be extracted from sands with a magnet. (See the pictures of lodestone on page 35.) It is widely distributed in igneous and metamorphic rocks and in veins.

Iron forms up to 72 per cent of magnetite by weight. The crystals have the symmetry of the cubic system. They have no cleavage. Magnetite also occurs in granular or massive forms. The specific gravity is 5·2 and the hardness is $5\frac{1}{2}-6\frac{1}{2}$. This black, opaque mineral has a shiny metallic to dull lustre. The streak is black. Magnetite is associated with iron-rich silicates, such as garnet, and also with amphiboles, epidote and pyroxene.

Hematite Fe_2O_3

By weight, iron forms about 70 per cent of hematite (or haematite). This mineral belongs to the trigonal crystal system. Hematite, called kidney ore, occurs in mamillated masses. This opaque mineral is often steel-grey to black, but it is reddish in compact and earthy forms. The streak is dark red to reddish-brown.

The specific gravity is 4·9—5·3 and the hardness is 5—6. This brittle mineral has no cleavage. Hematite occurs in igneous and metamorphic rocks and in hydrothermal veins. It is also found in some sedimentary rocks.

Goethite $FeO(OH)$

Crystals of goethite, belonging to the orthorhombic system, can be very beautiful. Goethite also occurs in botryoidal and stalactite-like forms

Manganese ores

Psilomelane

Goethite

Siderite

and it is sometimes earthy.

The specific gravity is 3·3—4·3 and the hardness is 5—5½. It is usually extremely dark brown. Earthy goethite is lighter. The lustre ranges from adamantine to dull. Goethite occurs in veins or as a precipitate.

Siderite $FeCO_3$

Iron forms only 48 per cent of siderite (chalybite), but it is easy to work and is a major source of iron. It occurs in hydrothermal veins and sedimentary rocks, in association with chalcopyrite, pyrite and galena.

The crystals have the symmetry of the trigonal system. Siderite also occurs in massive, granular, fibrous, botryoidal

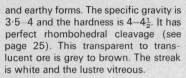

Pyrolusite

and earthy forms. The specific gravity is 3·5—4 and the hardness is 4—4½. It has perfect rhombohedral cleavage (see page 25). This transparent to translucent ore is grey to brown. The streak is white and the lustre vitreous.

Manganese Ores

Manganese is a grey metal of great importance in the steel industry. Two important manganese ores, psilomelane and pyrolusite, are oxides.

Psilomelane
Approx $BaMn_9O_{16}(OH)_4$

Psilomelane is a complex manganese and barium oxide, that belongs to the monoclinic crystal system. It occurs as crystals, as stalactite-like and as botryoidal forms. The specific gravity of this opaque, black to steel-grey mineral is 3·3—4·7 and the hardness is up to 6. It occurs in sediments and in quartz veins.

Pyrolusite MnO_2

Pyrolusite occurs in sedimentary rocks and quartz veins. It is associated with goethite and limonite. The rare crystals belong to the tetragonal system. Pyrolusite sometimes occurs in massive, rounded or branching forms. The mineral has perfect prismatic cleavage. It is opaque and black to bluish-grey, with a specific gravity of 4·5—5·1. The crystals have a hardness of 6.

Lead Ores

Lead resists corrosion, is easily shaped, and is used in such things as alloys and batteries. It also absorbs radiation and is often used to shield people from radioactive substances. The chief ore, galena, is a sulphide, while anglesite is a sulphate.

Galena PbS

Lead forms nearly 87 per cent of galena and, often, another 0·5 per cent is silver, so galena is also an ore of that rare metal. The shiny crystals, belonging to the cubic system, cleave perfectly into smaller cubes.

The specific gravity is 7·5–7·6 and the hardness is $2\frac{1}{2}$. This opaque, lead-grey mineral has a metallic lustre. It occurs in sedimentary rocks, often filling cavities in limestones and dolomites, and is sometimes associated with biotite, feldspar and garnet. It also occurs in pegmatites and, in hydrothermal veins, with chalcopyrite, pyrite and sphalerite.

Anglesite $PbSO_4$

Anglesite often encloses a mass of galena, from which it has formed. Anglesite belongs to the orthorhombic crystal system, and it often occurs in masses or as grains. The specific gravity is 6·3–6·4 and the hardness is 3. Usually colourless or white, anglesite may sometimes be shaded yellow, grey or blue. When pure, it has an adamantine lustre.

Zinc Ores

Zinc resembles lead, but it is harder and is used to plate other metals. The chief ore is sphalerite, which is also called zinc blende or blende. Sphalerite is a sulphide, while hemimorphite is a silicate.

Sphalerite ZnS

Sphalerite, an abundant mineral, often contains some iron. In hydrothermal veins, it is associated with galena and, in limestones, with pyrite and magnetite. The crystals, belonging to the cubic system, have perfect cleavage. Crystals are not rare, but this mineral also occurs in massive and fibrous forms. The specific gravity is 3·9–4·1 and the hardness is $3\frac{1}{2}$–$4\frac{1}{2}$. Although usually brown to black, the colour of this transparent to translucent mineral varies. Its name comes from the Greek *sphaleros*, meaning deceptive, because it may sometimes be confused with some other minerals. The lustre is resinous to adamantine.

Hemimorphite
$Zn_4Si_2O_7(OH)_2 . H_2O$

Hemimorphite is a transparent to translucent mineral with a vitreous

Lead ores

Galena
(Greece)

White crystals
of anglesite in
galena

Zinc ores

Sphalerite

Hemimorphite

Silver ore

Argentite (Mexico)

Nickel ore

Nickeline (South America)

lustre. Generally white, it may also be bluish, greenish or brownish. This mineral belongs to the orthorhombic system, and it also occurs in fibrous, rounded or massive forms. The specific gravity is 3·4—3·5 and the hardness is $4\frac{1}{2}$—5. In limestones, hemimorphite is associated with anglesite, galena and sphalerite.

Silver Ore: Argentite Ag_2S

Argentite, the main silver ore, contains about 87 per cent of that mineral. It is also called silver glance and is identical chemically with another mineral, acanthite. But acanthite crystallizes below 180°C (356°F) with the symmetry of the orthorhombic system, while argentite crystallizes at a higher temperature and its crystals belong to the cubic system. Argentite sometimes occurs in massive, tree-like or wiry forms. The specific gravity is 7·2—7·4 and the hardness is 2—$2\frac{1}{2}$. This lead-grey, opaque mineral has a shiny grey streak. It occurs in hydrothermal veins

and is often located in masses of galena.

Nickel Ore: Nickeline NiAs

Nickel, a silver-coloured metal, is used in alloys and for plating. One of the chief ores is the nickel arsenide nickeline (or niccolite). Crystals of nickeline, belonging to the hexagonal system, are rare. Nickeline usually occurs in masses. The specific gravity is 7·8 and the hardness is 5—$5\frac{1}{2}$. This opaque, pale copper-red mineral has a pale brownish-black streak. It occurs in igneous rocks, with chalcopyrite, and in hydrothermal veins, with silver and cobalt ores.

Copper ores

Azurite with malachite

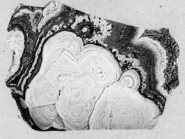

Malachite with azurite

Chalcopyrite

Copper Ores

Copper occurs as a native element (page 59), but most copper comes from ores, including two carbonates, azurite and malachite; three sulphides, chalcopyrite, bornite and chalcosine; and the oxide cuprite. The richest is cuprite (89 per cent copper), but chalcopyrite, which contains only 35 per cent copper, is the most common.

Azurite $Cu_3(CO_3)_2(OH)_2$

Azurite (or chessylite) can be identified by its azure-blue colour. It is sometimes interbanded with malachite, which is green. Azurite belongs to the monoclinic system. This mineral also occurs in massive, earthy and radiating forms. The specific gravity is 3·8 and the hardness is $3\frac{1}{2}$–4. The lustre of this transparent to translucent mineral is vitreous to adamantine. It dissolves in dilute hydrochloric acid. Azurite is a secondary copper mineral that has come from the altera-

tion of earlier copper minerals, by water and air.

Malachite $Cu_2CO_3(OH)_2$

Malachite is used as a semi-precious stone, and banded malachite with various shades of green makes beautiful ornaments. Malachite is a secondary copper mineral, often associated with azurite, cuprite and native copper.

Crystals of malachite, belonging to the monoclinic system, are rare. More often the mineral occurs in botryoidal and stalactite-like forms, or as crusts. It may also be earthy or granular. The specific gravity is 3·9–4·1 and the hardness, $3\frac{1}{2}$–4. Malachite dissolves in dilute hydrochloric acid.

Chalcopyrite $CuFeS_2$

Chalcopyrite (copper pyrites) is an opaque, brass-yellow mineral. It is softer than pyrite (page 24), but more brittle and harder than gold.

Crystals of chalcopyrite belong to the tetragonal system, but the mineral usually occurs in masses. The specific gravity is 4·1–4·3 and the hardness is $3\frac{1}{2}$–4. The streak is greenish-black. When a sample tarnishes, it may display iridescence (showing the rainbow colours). It dissolves in nitric acid. Chalcopyrite occurs as a primary (unaltered) mineral in igneous rocks and hydrothermal veins. It is associated with cassiterite, galena, pyrite and sphalerite. It also occurs in contact metamorphic rocks.

Bornite Cu_5FeS_4

Bornite is also called peacock ore because, when it tarnishes from reddish-brown to purple, it becomes vividly iridescent. The streak is pale grey to black. Bornite belongs to the cubic crystal system. Crystals are rare and the mineral occurs mostly in a massive form. This brittle, opaque mineral has a specific gravity of 5·1 and a hardness of 3. It dissolves in nitric acid. Bornite occurs in hydrothermal veins, being associated with chalcopyrite and chalcosine. It is also found in some pegmatites and hydrothermal deposits.

Chalcosine Cu_2S

Chalcosine (chalcocite or copper glance) is often associated with native copper and cuprite. The crystals, of the orthorhombic system, are rare, and the mineral usually occurs in massive or powdery forms. The specific gravity is 5·5–5·8 and the hardness is $2\frac{1}{2}$–3. This dark grey mineral tarnishes to black. It dissolves in hot nitric acid.

Cuprite Cu_2O

Cuprite (red copper ore) is a translucent, dark red mineral, similar to hematite (which is harder) and cinnabar (which is softer). It is usually a secondary mineral, found in the top layers of veins. It is often associated with azurite, chalcosine, native copper and malachite. Cuprite belongs to the cubic system, and it also occurs in massive or granular forms. The specific gravity is 6·1 and the hardness is $3\frac{1}{2}$–4. It has very poor cleavage and fractures unevenly.

Cuprite
(Arizona, USA)

Cubic crystals
of bornite
(Cornwall, England)

Chalcosine

Antimony Ore: Stibnite Sb_2S_3

The most common source of the metal antimony is the sulphide mineral stibnite (antimonite), although antimony may occur as a native element (see page 61). Antimony forms up to 71 per cent of stibnite. The crystals, belonging to the orthorhombic system, are often elongated. Needle-shaped crystals may form attractive, radiating groups. The crystals have perfect cleavage along their lengths. Stibnite may also be massive or granular.

The specific gravity is 4·6 and the hardness is 2. This opaque, lead-grey mineral crystallizes at low temperatures in hydrothermal veins, fills dissolved cavities in limestones and occurs in hot spring deposits. It is often associated with cinnabar, galena, orpiment, pyrite and realgar.

Tin Ore: Cassiterite SnO_2

Tin is an important metal used for plating, but tin cans are usually made of steel and coated with tin. The oxide cassiterite (or tinstone) is the chief ore. About 78 per cent of cassiterite is tin. The crystals have the symmetry of the tetragonal system. Cassiterite also occurs in massive, rounded or granular forms. Because they are heavy for their size, cassiterite pebbles become concentrated in alluvial deposits, forming 'stream tin'.

This reddish-brown to black mineral is sometimes yellowish. The streak is white, greyish or brownish. It is nearly transparent to opaque and it has an adamantine lustre. The specific gravity is 7 and the hardness is 6—7. Cassiterite forms in hydrothermal veins, and in pegmatites in and around granite. It is associated with bismuthinite, mica, quartz, topaz, tourmaline and wolframite.

Molybdenum Ore: Molybdenite MoS_2

Molybdenum is a metal used to make hard, resistant steels. It is also used in tools, drills and electrical equipment.

Antimony ore

Stibnite

Tin ore

Cassiterite

Molybdenum ore

Molybdenite (the dark mineral) with quartz and molybdite (yellow), Canada

The sulphide molybdenite is the main ore. About 60 per cent of the ore is molybdenum. The crystals belong to the hexagonal system and have perfect basal cleavage. The mineral usually occurs in leafy or scaly masses and in massive or granular forms.

The specific gravity is 4·6—4·7 and the hardness is 1—1½. This opaque, lead-grey mineral has a greenish-grey streak and a greasy feel. Graphite is similar, but it has a duller lustre and a lower specific gravity. Molybdenite occurs widely, but deposits are small. It is found in granites and in

cubic system and have perfect cubic cleavage. Cobaltite also occurs in masses, as grains in metamorphic rocks, or in hydrothermal veins, being associated with nickeline. The specific gravity is 6·3 and the hardness is 5½. This opaque mineral is white to grey, often with a reddish shade. The streak is grey to black.

Mercury Ore: Cinnabar HgS
Mercury is a silvery metal which is unusual because it is liquid at ordinary temperatures. It is used in electrical and scientific instruments, such as

Cobalt ore

Cobaltite

Mercury ore

Cinnabar

contact metamorphic rocks, where it is associated with garnet, pyrite, pyroxenes, scheelite and tourmaline. In veins, minerals associated with molybdenite include cassiterite, fluorite, scheelite and wolframite.

Cobalt Ore: Cobaltite CoAsS
The metal cobalt is used in alloys and in pigments. The chief ore is the sulphide cobaltite. Its name comes from the German *kobold*, or *demon*, because miners once thought it a harmful and mischievous metal. In fact, it does give off poisonous arsenic fumes when heated. The crystals belong to the

thermometers, and in chemicals and paints. The chief ore is the poisonous sulphide cinnabar, 86 per cent of which is mercury. Cinnabar is a scarlet to brownish-red, transparent to translucent mineral. It has a vermilion streak. The rare adamantine crystals belong to the trigonal system. Cinnabar is commonly found in dull massive or granular forms. The specific gravity is 8—8·1 and the hardness is 2—2½.

Cinnabar occurs in volcanic areas, around hot springs and in fissures in sedimentary rocks. It is associated with baryte, calcite, chalcedony, pyrite, quartz, realgar and stibnite.

Arsenic Ore: Orpiment As_2S_3

Although it occurs as a native element (see pages 60–1), arsenic comes mostly from ores, including the sulphide orpiment. This golden to brownish or reddish-yellow mineral is found in hydrothermal veins and in hot spring deposits. It often occurs with realgar (AsS), a similar, red to orange mineral. Orpiment crystals, which are rare, belong to the monoclinic system. Orpiment is usually massive. This transparent to translucent mineral has a resinous to pearly lustre. The specific gravity is 3·5 and the hardness is $1\frac{1}{2}$–2.

Titanium Ore: Rutile TiO_2

Titanium, a strong, light, silver-grey metal, resists corrosion. It is used in the steel industry. The oxide, rutile, is a major ore. The crystals, belonging to the tetragonal system, are usually elongated, with parallel lines on their sides. Needle-like crystals occur in quartz veins. Twinning is quite common (see page 32). The specific gravity is 4·2–4·4 and the hardness is 6–$6\frac{1}{2}$. Rutile is usually reddish-brown, but it may be yellowish-red or black. The lustre is adamantine but dark varieties are metallic. Rutile occurs in igneous and metamorphic rocks. Fragments are found in beach sands and alluvial deposits.

Tungsten Ore: Wolframite $(Fe,Mn)WO_4$

Tungsten, a metal used in the steel industry, has an extremely high melting point, 3410°C (6170°F), making it suitable for filaments in electric light bulbs. The iron-manganese tungstate, wolframite, is the main ore.

The crystals, of the monoclinic system, may be tabular or elongated. Wolframite also occurs in massive or granular forms. The specific gravity is 7–7·5 and the hardness is 4–$4\frac{1}{2}$. This opaque, grey-black to brownish-black mineral occurs in pegmatites and in hydrothermal veins. It is often

Arsenic ore

Orpiment with realgar

Titanium ore

Rutile

Rutile needles in quartz

Tungsten ore

Wolframite (the dark mineral) with mica (top) and quartz

Chromium ore

Chromite (Greece)

Uranium ore

Uraninite (Cornwall, England)

found with cassiterite, galena, quartz, sphalerite and tourmaline.

Chromium Ore: Chromite $FeCr_2O_4$
Chromium, another metal used in the steel industry, is also important for plating. The only ore is the oxide chromite. Chromite usually occurs in massive or granular forms. The cubic crystals are fairly rare. The specific gravity is $4 \cdot 1 - 5 \cdot 1$ and the hardness is $5\frac{1}{2}$. This opaque, black to brownish-black mineral resembles magnetite. Chromite is only slightly magnetic and has a brown streak. It occurs in igneous rocks and alluvial deposits.

Bismuth Ore: Bismuthinite Bi_2S_3
Bismuth is a metal which occurs as a native element (see page 61). One important ore is the sulphide bismuthinite (bismuth glance). This mineral belongs to the orthorhombic system. It is usually massive, leaf-like or fibrous. The specific gravity is $6 \cdot 8$ and the hardness is 2. This light grey, opaque mineral has a metallic lustre. It dissolves in nitric acid. It occurs in hydrothermal veins and in igneous rocks. It is associated with chalcopyrite, galena, magnetite, pyrite, sphalerite, and tin and tungsten ores.

Uranium Ore: Uraninite UO_2
Uranium, a radioactive element, is used as a fuel in atomic power stations. The chief ore is the oxide uraninite, which also contains some radium and polonium. Massive forms of uraninite are called pitchblende, but the mineral may also be botryoidal or earthy. Crystals, of the cubic system, are rare. The specific gravity of the crystals is $7 \cdot 5 - 10$, but it ranges between $6 \cdot 5$ and 9 for pitchblende. The hardness is $5 - 6$. This opaque, brownish-black to black mineral occurs in pegmatites, often with tourmaline and zircon. Pitchblende occurs in hydrothermal veins, with cassiterite, chalcopyrite, galena and pyrite. It also occurs in some alluvial deposits.

Other Oxides

Besides those already described under ores, there are other oxides which are not metal ores. They include spinel, chrysoberyl and corundum. Varieties of these hard minerals are precious and semi-precious gemstones.

Spinel $MgAl_2O_4$

Spinel occurs in a wide variety of colours, including black, blue, brown, green and, rarely, colourless. The most common colour is scarlet (or ruby spinel). In the past, ruby spinel was often mistaken for true ruby, a variety of corundum. For example, the Black Prince ruby in the British Imperial State Crown, shown on page 39, is really a spinel.

Spinel is usually translucent, but specimens range from nearly opaque to transparent. The crystals have the symmetry of the cubic system and they often have eight faces. They have a vitreous lustre and no cleavage. The streak is white. Spinel also occurs in massive forms. The hardness is $7\frac{1}{2}$–8 and the specific gravity is 3·6. Spinel is found in igneous rocks, such as gabbro, and also in metamorphosed limestones and shales. It also occurs in river gravels.

The term spinel is also applied to a group of minerals, which includes spinel as a specific member. This is because manganese, iron and zinc may substitute for the magnesium. Members of the spinel group include the black galaxite (manganese aluminium oxide), which has a specific gravity of 4; the black iron type, hercynite, which has a specific gravity of 4·4; and the dark, blue-green gahnite, with a specific gravity of 4·6. The streak varies from brown (galaxite) to green (hercynite) and grey (gahnite). Chromite (see page 73) is also a member of the spinel group.

Chrysoberyl $BeAl_2O_4$

Chrysoberyl has a hardness of $8\frac{1}{2}$ and is the third hardest mineral after diamond and corundum. Its hardness distinguishes it from olivine, which it sometimes resembles. The crystals have the symmetry of the orthorhombic system and are usually tabular. Twinning is common. Chrysoberyl also occurs in massive and granular forms. This transparent to translucent mineral occurs in shades of green and yellow. The lustre is vitreous.

One emerald-green gemstone variety, alexandrite, turns red in artificial light. Other gemstone varieties contain an internal fibrous structure of fine parallel lines. As you rotate these varieties, the lustre changes, like that seen in a cat's eye. This effect is called *chatoyancy* and cat's eye is the name of this variety.

Chrysoberyl is found in granite pegmatites and mica schists. Because they are hard, worn fragments of chrysoberyl often accumulate in alluvial deposits.

Spinel (the dark mineral) with calcite and quartz

A cut and polished chrysoberyl

Corundum (North Carolina, USA)

Sapphire in basalt (Germany)

Ruby in chrome zoisite (East Africa)

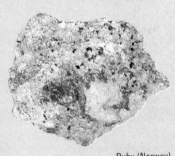
Ruby (Norway)

Corundum Al_2O_3

Corundum is a common, rather dull, transparent to translucent mineral, distinguished by its hardness of 9. It is mostly bluish-grey to brown in colour. However, two rare varieties, the pigeon's blood (red) ruby, coloured by the presence of some chrome in the structure, and the cornflower-blue sapphire, possibly coloured by iron or titanium, are among the most prized of gemstones. Fine green specimens are called Oriental emeralds; violet kinds are called Oriental amethysts; and yellow ones, Oriental topazes. But all the gemstones are rare. Much more common is its occurrence as a greyish-black rock called emery. Emery, which is used as an abrasive, is not a mineral, because it contains some magnetite, hematite and spinel.

Crystals of corundum have the symmetry of the trigonal system. They may be barrel-shaped, spindle-shaped or tabular. They have no cleavage. Some prized rubies and sapphires contain three sets of internal parallel fibres, crossing each other at about 60°. It is possible to cut these specimens so that they appear as six-rayed stars. This property is called *asterism.* Corundum also occurs in massive and granular forms.

The specific gravity of corundum is 4. The streak is white and the lustre adamantine to vitreous. Corundum is found in pegmatites and syenites which contain little silica, but it mostly occurs in metamorphic rocks, such as gneiss, marble and schist. Fragments of this hard mineral are also found in alluvial deposits.

Halides

Halides contain one of the so-called halogen elements, chlorine, bromine, iodine or fluorine. Halite and fluorite are common halide minerals.

Halite NaCl

Halite is rock salt. It formed mostly when enclosed seas dried up. Salt domes form when layers of halite are compressed and rise up through overlying layers of sediments. These domes may be traps for oil which has penetrated through the rocks. Crystals of halite have the symmetry of the cubic system and, when struck, they break into tiny cubes. Halite also occurs in massive, granular and compact forms. The specific gravity is 2·1—2·2 and the hardness is $2\frac{1}{2}$. This transparent, colourless or white mineral may be tinted blue, red or yellow by impurities. The lustre is vitreous. Halite is soluble in water.

Halite

Kinds of fluorite

Fluorite CaF_2

Fluorite (or fluorspar) is a widely-distributed mineral. It is found in hydrothermal veins, in association with baryte, galena, quartz and sphalerite. The crystals, belonging to the cubic system, have perfect octahedral cleavage. Fluorite may also be compact or granular. The specific gravity is 3·2 and the hardness is 4. Colours vary greatly and a single crystal may have more than one colour in it. Common colours include blue, brown, green, purple and yellow. Colourless crystals and other colours also occur. A colourful, banded variety, called Blue John, is found in Derbyshire, England. This transparent to translucent mineral has a vitreous lustre. Fluorite dissolves in sulphuric acid.

Fluorite

Detail from the above sample

Blue John

Dolomite

Carbonates

There are 70 or so carbonates. Two of them, calcite and dolomite, are common rock-forming minerals.

Calcite $CaCO_3$

Calcite occurs in some igneous intrusions, sedimentary limestones and in metamorphic marbles. It is often precipitated from seawater. In caves, it forms stalactites and stalagmites and, around hot springs, it forms travertine and tufa. The crystals, of the trigonal system, are very varied. They may be rhombohedral, tabular, elongated, stalactite-like, and so on. Nail-head spar is a variety popular with collectors. It has prismatic crystals topped by flat rhombohedrons. The specific gravity is 2·7 and the hardness is 3. Calcite is mostly colourless or white, but impurities cause many colour shades. Pure Iceland spar displays double refraction (see page 27). This transparent to translucent mineral has a vitreous to earthy lustre. It dissolves readily in cold dilute hydrochloric acid.

Dolomite $CaMg(CO_3)_2$

Dolomite is similar to calcite, but it dissolves only slowly in cold hydrochloric acid. It is found in hydrothermal veins, in some igneous rocks, and as an evaporite or through the alteration of limestones. The crystals, of the trigonal system, are usually rhombohedral, with perfect cleavage. It also occurs in massive, granular and compact forms. The specific gravity is 2·8–2·9 and the hardness is $3\frac{1}{2}$–4. This transparent to translucent mineral is generally white or honey-coloured. The lustre is vitreous to pearly.

Kinds of calcite

Calcite

Sulphates

Sulphates, the salts of sulphuric acid, contain SO_4 in their chemical formulae. They are mainly evaporites or they may form in volcanic regions. Common sulphates include baryte, anhydrite, gypsum and epsomite.

Baryte $BaSO_4$

Baryte (barytes or barite) is the main source of barium, which is used in medicine. It is also used to make paints and some kinds of paper, but most of it is used as drilling mud for the oil industry.

The crystals, of the orthorhombic system, may be tabular or elongated, and it forms the cement in some sandstones.

Anhydrite $CaSO_4$

Anhydrite, a source of sulphur, is used to make fertilizers, plaster and cement. Crystals, belonging to the orthorhombic system, are rare. They have three good cleavages, at right angles to each other. The mineral also occurs in massive, granular and fibrous forms. The specific gravity is $2 \cdot 9 - 3$ and the hardness is $3 - 3\frac{1}{2}$. This transparent to opaque mineral is colourless to white. Massive varieties are often bluish and other kinds are brown or red. The streak is white and the lustre

Kinds of baryte

Crystalline baryte

Fibrous baryte

with perfect basal cleavage. The mineral also occurs in layered, fibrous and cockscomb-like masses. Baryte may also be granular or stalactite-like. It has a high specific gravity (4·5) which helps to distinguish it from calcite or dolomite. The hardness is $3 - 3\frac{1}{2}$. This transparent to opaque mineral is usually white or colourless. But coloured varieties also occur. The lustre is vitreous. A flame is coloured green by baryte. It does not dissolve in dilute acids. It is found in hydrothermal veins, in cavities in limestones,

Anhydrite

vitreous to pearly. Anhydrite does not dissolve readily in dilute acids. It is associated with gypsum and halite. It may form from gypsum, when gypsum loses its water. Some occurs above salt domes and, rarely, it is found in veins.

Gypsum $CaSO_4 . 2H_2O$

Gypsum, the commonest sulphate, is used to make plaster of Paris. The crystals, of the monoclinic system, may be tabular or elongated. Fibrous, massive and granular forms also occur. The specific gravity is 2·3—2·4 and the hardness is 2. Gypsum is transparent to translucent and usually colourless or white, but shades of brown and yellow occur. The lustre is vitreous to pearly and gypsum dissolves in hydrochloric acid. The colourless, transparent variety is called selenite. The fibrous kind is called satin spar and the massive granular form is alabaster. Gypsum is precipitated from seawater with halite. It also forms in volcanic regions or when anhydrite takes up water. Desert roses are platy crystal rosettes of gypsum enclosing grains of sand. They are precipitated from ground water.

Epsomite $MgSO_4 . 7H_2O$

Epsomite (Epsom salts) dissolves in

Kinds of gypsum

Gypsum (selenite)

Gypsum desert rose (Africa)

Epsomite

water, giving it a bitter taste. It occurs in mineral water and is precipitated when the water evaporates. It forms in volcanic regions and on the walls of caves and mines where magnesium-rich rocks are exposed. Crystals, of the orthorhombic system, have one perfect cleavage. But epsomite usually occurs in botryoidal and delicate fibrous crusts. The specific gravity is 1·7 and the hardness is $2—2\frac{1}{2}$. Epsomite is colourless to white and transparent to translucent. The lustre is vitreous to silky or earthy.

Apatite (Canada)

Phosphates and Vanadates

Phosphates and vanadates form groups of minerals that are similar to one another. Phosphates are compounds containing phosphorus, with PO_4 in their chemical formulae. They include apatite, which is the most common, pyromorphite and turquoise. Vanadates are compounds containing the element vanadium, with VO_4 in the formulae. Vanadinite and carnotite are vanadates.

Apatite $Ca_5(PO_4)_3(F,Cl,OH)$

Apatite is a major source of phosphates, which are used to make fertilizers. Superphosphates contain apatite which has been treated with sulphuric acid. Apatite is a fairly complex mineral. Fluorine (F), chlorine (Cl) and hydroxyl (OH) can substitute for each other and the varieties of apatite are determined by the amounts of these substances they contain. In the past, apatite was often confused with other minerals. Its name comes from the Greek, *apate*, meaning 'deceit'.

Crystals of apatite have the symmetry of the hexagonal system. They may be column-like or tabular. Apatite also occurs in massive, granular and earthy forms. The specific gravity is 3·1–3·4 and the hardness is 5. This transparent to opaque mineral is commonly some shade of green. Other

Turquoise (blue) in trachyte (New Mexico, USA)

colours, including blue, brown, grey, red and violet, also occur and some kinds are colourless. Some beautiful specimens are used in ornaments, but apatite is too soft for jewellery. The streak is white and the lustre vitreous. Apatite dissolves in hydrochloric acid.

Small crystals of apatite are found in a wide range of igneous rocks and large crystals occur in granite pegmatites and hydrothermal veins. The mineral is also found in metamorphic and sedimentary rocks.

Pyromorphite $Pb_5(PO_4)_3Cl$

Pyromorphite is a minor ore of lead

Pyromorphite

and is found as a secondary (altered) mineral in veins containing such lead ores as galena and anglesite.

The crystals belong to the hexagonal system. They are column-like and often barrel-shaped. Pyromorphite also occurs in fibrous, granular or globular masses. This subtransparent to translucent mineral is generally green or brown. More rarely, colourless, orange, white and yellow types are found. The streak is white and the lustre resinous to subadamantine. The specific gravity is 6·5–7·1 and the hardness is $3\frac{1}{2}$–4. It dissolves in hydrochloric and nitric acid.

Vanadinite (orange) with calcite
(New Mexico, USA)

Turquoise
$CuAl_6(PO_4)_4(OH)_8 \cdot 5H_2O$

Sky-blue specimens of turquoise are popular semi-precious stones. But many are discoloured by sunlight and they may turn green if exposed to water or grease. Turquoise crystals, of the triclinic system, are tiny and rare. The mineral usually occurs in massive, granular or crusty forms. The specific gravity is 2·6 and the hardness is 5–6. The crystals are transparent, but massive varieties are opaque. Turquoise may also be bluish-green to greenish-grey. The streak is white or greenish. Massive varieties have a waxy lustre. The crystals are vitreous. Turquoise is a secondary mineral. It occurs in veins in association with igneous and sedimentary rocks which contain aluminium.

Vanadinite $Pb_5(VO_4)_3Cl$

Vanadinite was once a major ore of the metal vanadium, which is used in the steel industry, but vanadium is now obtained as a by-product of some iron ores and bauxite. Crystals of vanadinite, belonging to the hexagonal system, are often column-like and sharp. Rounded forms also occur. The specific gravity is 6·7–7·1 and the hardness is 3. This transparent to nearly opaque mineral may be orange-red or brown to yellow. The streak is white to yellowish and the lustre

resinous. Vanadinite is a rare secondary mineral, associated with lead ores.

Carnotite $K_2(UO_2)_2(VO_4)_2 \cdot 3H_2O$

Carnotite, an ore of uranium, occurs in sedimentary rocks. It is deposited by ground water that has been in contact with uranium and vanadium minerals. The crystals, with the symmetry of the monoclinic system, are rare. More usually, carnotite is powdery, as in the photograph on this page. The specific gravity is 4–5 and the hardness is 2. This bright yellow to greenish-yellow mineral has a dull lustre. Carnotite dissolves in hydrochloric and nitric acids.

Carnotite (Utah, USA)

Silicates

Oxygen and silicon are the commonest elements in the Earth's crust. The silicates are chemical combinations of oxygen and silicon, together with one or more other elements, principally aluminium, iron, calcium, sodium, potassium and magnesium, the other common elements in the Earth's crust (see page 12), although other less common elements also occur.

The silica group (see pages 94–9) includes minerals that are basically silicon dioxide, that is, they consist of oxygen and silicon only. Minerals of the silica group, including quartz, are sometimes classified as oxides, but many scientists regard them as silicates. The silicates, including the minerals of the silica group, form about 95 per cent of the Earth's crust. Important silicates are described on pages 82–101 of this Guide.

Olivine $(Mg,Fe)_2SiO_4$

Olivine is the name for a group of minerals, which are silicates of magnesium and iron, with the above chemical formula. Olivine is named after the green colour of olives. But it is sometimes yellowish or brownish to black. When olivine weathers, its surface often turns reddish-brown.

Olivine crystals belong to the orthorhombic system (see the diagram on page 31), but well-developed crystals are rare. Olivine is brittle and, when it is split, it fractures irregularly. Grains of olivine, resembling bits of green glass, are scattered through some igneous rocks. Olivine also occurs in granular masses. The mineral has a hardness of $6\frac{1}{2}$–7 and common olivine has a specific gravity of about 3·4. Its lustre is vitreous and its streak is white or grey.

Olivine is an important rock-forming mineral. It occurs in basic to ultrabasic (silica-poor) igneous rocks, including basalt, gabbro and peridotite, which is especially rich in olivine (see pages 102–3). Dunite is a rock

Olivine in volcanic rock (France)

Zircon (Canada)

composed almost entirely of olivine. Some marble contains a magnesium-rich form of olivine, called forsterite. The iron-rich variety is called fayalite. Olivine does not usually occur in sediments, because it is unstable in water. It is found in basaltic Moon rocks and in stony and stony-iron meteorites (pages 122–3).

Peridot

This light green, transparent gem is a form of olivine. Its oily, vitreous lustre distinguishes it from other green gems. It was used in the Middle Ages as a decoration for church robes and plates. It is now used in earrings, pendants, and so on.

Zircon $ZrSiO_4$

Zircon is a source of the metal zirconium. This metal withstands high temperatures and so it is often used in rocket engines and high-temperature furnaces. The mineral zircon often occurs as well-formed crystals that belong to the tetragonal system. Crystals occur widely in igneous rocks, including granite and syenite, and in such metamorphic rocks as gneisses and schists. Zircon is fairly hard and heavy. Its hardness is $7\frac{1}{2}$ and its specific gravity is $4{\cdot}6{-}4{\cdot}7$. When it is eroded out of igneous and meta-morphic rocks, it is washed into sands, where it occurs as worn grains.

Commonly, zircon is brownish in colour. There are also colourless, grey, yellow and green varieties, but synthetically-made zircons are sometimes blue. The streak is white. Zircons are transparent to translucent. The lustre ranges from adamantine to vitreous. Transparent and adamantine zircons are used as substitutes for diamonds in jewellery. But zircon is brittle and the edges of a stone set in a ring may be chipped off.

Sphene $CaTiSiO_5$

The name sphene comes from the Greek word for wedge. It has this name because its crystals, which belong to the monoclinic system, are often flattened and wedge-shaped. Besides occurring as crystals, sphene is also found in massive forms. Sphene is sometimes called titanite.

The mineral has a specific gravity of $3{\cdot}4{-}3{\cdot}6$ and a hardness of 5. The lustre is adamantine to resinous. Brilliant, transparent varieties are sometimes used as gems. They can be very fiery. But other varieties may be nearly opaque. Commonly, sphene is brown or greenish-yellow, but other colours occur. Sphene is found in coarse-grained igneous rocks, such as syenites and associated pegmatites, and in such metamorphic rocks as gneiss and schist.

Zircon crystals

Sphene (Canada)

Crystal twins of sphene (Switzerland)

Garnets

Garnets are a group of minerals. They are compounds of silica and two other elements. But the varieties closely resemble one another. Garnets often occur as well-developed crystals that have the symmetry of the cubic system. The specific gravity is $3 \cdot 6 - 4 \cdot 3$ and the hardness is $6 - 7\frac{1}{2}$. These transparent to translucent minerals are used as gemstones and abrasives. They occur in such metamorphic rocks as schists and gneisses, in some igneous rocks, and also in rocks from the Earth's mantle. Weathered garnets are found in sands.

Almandine ($Fe_3Al_2Si_3O_{12}$) is a red to almost black garnet. One type, rhodolite, is rose-red to purple. Andradite ($Ca_3Fe_2Si_3O_{12}$) may be green, brown or yellow to black in colour. A brilliant emerald-green type, demantoid, is a prized gem. Melanites are black andradites. Grossular garnet ($Ca_3Al_2Si_3O_{12}$) may be brown to pale green or white. Hessonites are yellow and brown varieties. Pyrope ($Mg_3Al_2Si_3O_{12}$) is a popular, ruby-red gemstone. Spessartine ($Mn_3Al_2Si_3O_{12}$) has colours similar to almandine. Uvarovite ($Ca_3Cr_2Si_3O_{12}$) is a fairly rare, green garnet.

Kinds of garnet

Spessartine in rhyolite (Colorado, USA)

Almandine in mica schist (Alaska, USA)

Andradite with calcite (Norway)

Grossular

Uvarovite (dark green) with pyroxene and calcite (Canada)

Andalusite

Sillimanite (Bucholzite variety)

Kyanite (Massachusetts, USA)

Andalusite, Sillimanite, Kyanite

Some groups of minerals with the same chemical formula may have different structures and properties. For example, andalusite, sillimanite and kyanite have the same formula, Al_2SiO_5, but their densities and refractive indices differ. Kyanite also belongs to a different crystal system from the other two. Minerals with the same formula but different structures are said to exhibit polymorphism.

These three minerals commonly occur in metamorphic rocks. But andalusite, the least dense mineral, was formed at fairly low pressures, while kyanite, the densest, was formed by far greater pressures.

Andalusite

Andalusite forms crystals which belong to the orthorhombic system. One variety, called chiastolite, contains a cross-shaped pattern in a cross-section of the crystal. The cross is formed by clayey or carbonaceous material. The hardness varies from $6\frac{1}{2}$ to $7\frac{1}{2}$ and the specific gravity is $3.1-3.2$. Andalusite is usually pink or red. But some crystals are brown, green or grey. A transparent green variety is used as a gemstone.

Sillimanite

Crystals of sillimanite (or fibrolite) belong to the orthorhombic system. But it often occurs in fibrous or interwoven masses. The hardness is $6\frac{1}{2}-7\frac{1}{2}$ and the specific gravity is $3.2-3.3$. Sillimanite is colourless to white, yellow or brown.

Kyanite

Kyanite crystals belong to the triclinic system, often resembling flat blades. The specific gravity is $3.5-3.7$, but the hardness varies. Another name for kyanite is disthene, which means 'double strength'. It is so-called because, along the side of the crystal, the hardness is $5\frac{1}{2}$, while across it, the hardness is $6-7$. Colours are usually blue to white, but some crystals are grey or green.

85

Staurolite
$(Fe,Mg)_2(Al,Fe)_9Si_4O_{22}(O,OH)_2$

Staurolite gets its name from two Greek words, *stauros*, meaning cross, and *lithos* (stone). It is so-called because its crystals, which have the symmetry of the monoclinic system, are often twinned, forming a cross or an X-shape. Staurolite has a hardness of $7-7\frac{1}{2}$ and a specific gravity of $3\cdot7-3\cdot8$. The colour ranges from reddish to blackish-brown and the streak is grey. It is translucent to nearly opaque. The lustre is vitreous to resinous. It occurs in metamorphic rocks, with garnet, kyanite and mica.

Staurolite

Topaz (Maine, USA)

Epidote (France)

Topaz $Al_2SiO_4(OH,F)_2$
Topaz is a popular gemstone. Although generally thought of as yellow, topaz may be colourless, pale yellow, pale blue, greenish or, rarely, red or pink. This transparent to translucent mineral has a vitreous lustre. The column-like crystals, of the orthorhombic system, occur in cavities in some granites and rhyolites, and in quartz veins. It is associated with apatite, beryl, cassiterite, fluorite and tourmaline. The hardness is 8 and the specific gravity, $3\cdot5-3\cdot6$.

Epidote $Ca_2(Al,Fe)_3Si_3O_{12}(OH)$
Epidote is commonly green, but it may be yellowish-green to black. It often occurs as small crystals which belong to the monoclinic system. This transparent to nearly opaque mineral has perfect cleavage parallel to the length of the crystal. Epidote is found in metamorphic rocks and in veins in igneous rocks. It has a vitreous lustre, a hardness of $6-7$ and a specific gravity of $3\cdot2-3\cdot5$.

Beryl $Be_3Al_2Si_6O_{18}$
Beryl, a transparent to translucent mineral, may be green, blue, yellow or pink. The vivid green crystals of one variety, emerald, are the most

Beryl in feldspar
(New Hampshire, USA)

prized. The green or bluish-green aquamarine, the yellow heliodor and the pink morganite are also gemstones. Beryl belongs to the hexagonal crystal system. The hardness is $7\frac{1}{2}$–8 and the specific gravity is 2·6–2·8. The lustre is vitreous. Beryl occurs in cavities in granites and in some gneisses and schists, being associated with chrysoberyl and rutile.

Cordierite $(Mg,Fe)_2Al_4Si_5O_{18}$

Cordierite is a dark to greyish-blue, transparent to translucent mineral. Its crystals belong to the orthorhombic system. The hardness is 7 and the specific gravity, 2·5–2·8, increasing with the iron content. Cordierite occurs in metamorphic rocks, with andalusite, biotite, quartz and spinel.

Tourmaline $Na(Mg,Fe,Li,Al,Mn)_3Al_6(BO_3)_3Si_6O_{18}(OH,F)_4$

Tourmaline is one of the most complex of all silicates. It is usually black (when it is called schorl), or bluish-black. Other varieties include achroite (colourless), indicolite (blue), verdelite (green) and rubellite (pink and red). Blue, green and pink varieties are used as gemstones. The crystals, of the trigonal system, are often column- or needle-like. Tourmaline has a specific gravity of 3–3·2 and the hardness is 7. The lustre is vitreous. Tourmaline occurs in granites and some metamorphic rocks.

Cordierite

Stumpy crystals of tourmaline in quartz and apatite (Devon, England)

Emeralds

Aquamarine

Rubellite variety of tourmaline (California, USA)

Hypersthene

Pyroxenes

Pyroxenes are a widespread group of rock-forming silicates. A few varieties are used in jewellery and for ornaments. Pyroxenes occur in many igneous and some metamorphic rocks. Besides silica, they may contain one or more of the following elements: aluminium, calcium, iron, lithium, magnesium, sodium, and sometimes manganese or titanium.

Pyroxenes have good cleavage in two directions. The cleavages are almost at right angles to each other. This is one of the features that distinguishes them from the similar amphiboles (see pages 90–1), where the angle of cleavage is about 120°. Examples of pyroxenes include hypersthene, augite, aegirine, jadeite and spodumene. It is often difficult to tell one kind of pyroxene from another, except by chemical analysis or by detailed examination under a microscope.

Hypersthene (Mg,Fe)SiO₃

Hypersthene $(Mg,Fe)SiO_3$

This fairly dense and hard mineral has a specific gravity of 3·4–3·6 and a hardness of 5–6. Its crystals, which are rare, belong to the orthorhombic system. Apart from cleavage, hypersthene is also distinguished by its pale green to dark brownish- or greenish-black colouring. The streak is white or grey. The lustre is vitreous. One variety, bronzite, has a bronze lustre. Hypersthene occurs in igneous rocks, such as gabbro and some volcanic rocks, and stony meteorites.

Augite (Ca,Mg,Fe,Ti,Al)₂(Si,Al)₂O₆

Augite $(Ca,Mg,Fe,Ti,Al)_2(Si,Al)_2O_6$

Augite is the commonest pyroxene. It occurs as crystals, which have the symmetry of the monoclinic system, in igneous rocks, such as basalts and gabbros. Augite is brown, green or, often, black. The lustre is vitreous and the streak is white or grey. The specific gravity is 3–3·5, increasing according to the iron content. The hardness of augite is 5–6.

Augite from the crater of the Italian volcano, Stromboli

Aegirine (Arkansas, USA)

Aegirine NaFeSi₂O₆

Aegirine $NaFeSi_2O_6$

Aegirine is a less common pyroxene. It is named after a Scandinavian god of the sea, called Aegir. It is found in sodium-rich rocks, such as syenites, and associated pegmatites. The slender, elongated crystals belong to the monoclinic system. The specific gravity is 3·5–3·6 and the hardness is 6. This subtransparent to opaque mineral is dark green or brown to nearly black. The streak is grey and the lustre is vitreous.

Jadeite $NaAlSi_2O_6$

Jadeite is one of the two minerals used, especially in China, to make superb jade ornaments and statues. The other mineral is nephrite (see page 90). Jadeite, however, is rarer than nephrite and is more highly prized. Jadeite is a tough, translucent mineral with a vitreous lustre. It is usually light or dark green, but white, lilac and other colours also occur.

Jadeite

Spodumene

The hardness is $6-6\frac{1}{2}$ and the specific gravity is $3 \cdot 2 - 3 \cdot 4$. Crystals of jadeite, belonging to the monoclinic system, are rare. Jadeite occurs in metamorphic and some volcanic rocks.

Spodumene $LiAlSi_2O_6$

Two varieties of spodumene are used as gemstones. One is a rare, emerald-green variety, called hiddenite. The other is kunzite, a pinkish-lilac variety. Both are brittle and may be flawed if they are dropped.

Common spodumene is usually white or greyish-white in colour. This transparent to translucent mineral has a vitreous lustre. Crystals are sometimes enormous, being more than 12 metres (39 ft) long and weighing many tonnes. The crystals belong to the monoclinic system. The hardness is $6\frac{1}{2}-7$ and the specific gravity is 3–3.2. Spodumene occurs in granite pegmatites. Associated minerals include beryl and tourmaline.

Wollastonite $CaSiO_3$

Wollastonite was named after a British chemist, W. H. Wollaston (1766–1828). This calcium silicate is used in paints and ceramics. A white to grey mineral, wollastonite is subtransparent to translucent. It has a vitreous lustre, but fibrous varieties are rather silky. The hardness is $4\frac{1}{2}-5$ and the specific gravity $2 \cdot 8 - 3 \cdot 1$. The crystals belong to the triclinic system.

Wollastonite occurs when limestone or marble are metamorphosed together with silica-rich minerals, especially quartz. But, if iron or magnesium are present, one of the pyroxenes will form instead. Wollastonite is associated with calcite, epidote and tremolite, which it resembles (page 90). However, wollastonite dissolves in hydrochloric acid, while tremolite does not react.

Wollastonite

Anthophyllite
(Pennsylvania, USA)

Tremolite
(New York, USA)

Amphiboles

Amphiboles are another important group of rock-forming silicates. They are similar to pyroxenes (see page 88) and, like them, they occur widely in igneous and metamorphic rocks. Amphiboles also have good cleavage in two directions. But the angle between the cleavages is about 120°, not 90° as in the pyroxenes. Chemically, the amphiboles are complicated minerals, as can be seen from their formulae. A special feature is that water is chemically combined in amphiboles. Amphiboles include anthophyllite; the tremolite-actinolite series, which includes the variety nephrite; the glaucophane-riebeckite series, which includes the variety crocidolite; and hornblende.

Anthophyllite
$(Mg,Fe)_7Si_8O_{22}(OH)_2$
Anthophyllite gets its name from the Latin *anthophyllum*, meaning clove. Some specimens are clove-brown, but others are white or grey. The streak is white. Crystals, which are rare, have the symmetry of the orthorhombic system. But anthophyllite often occurs in a fibrous form. The lustre of the crystals is vitreous, but fibrous forms are silky. The mineral occurs in metamorphic, not igneous rocks. The hardness is 6 and the specific gravity increases from 2·8 to 3·4,

according to the iron content. The mineral is used in asbestos cement.

Tremolite, Actinolite $Ca_2(Mg,Fe)_5Si_8O_{22}(OH)_2$

Tremolite and actinolite are two similar minerals found in metamorphic rocks. They form a chemical series, as there can be a continuous variation in the amount of iron replacing magnesium. Tremolite contains little or no iron, but actinolite is iron-rich. Both may form elongated crystals, which belong to the monoclinic system, or they may occur as fibrous masses. Tremolite is an asbestos mineral used in insulation. The hardness is 5—6 and the specific gravity increases from 3 to 3·4, accord-

Crocidolite:
a variety of
riebeckite
(South Africa)

Actinolite

Nephrite (Rhode Island, USA)

ing to the iron content. These transparent to translucent minerals have a vitreous lustre. Tremolite is usually white to grey, while actinolite is light to dark green. The streak is white.

Nephrite, or greenstone, is a compact, tough variety of tremolite or actinolite. It is the more common kind of jade (see jadeite on page 89). The word nephrite comes from the Greek *nephros*, meaning kidney, because people once believed that amulets of nephrite protected them against kidney complaints.

Glaucophane, Riebeckite
$Na_2(Mg,Fe,Al)_5Si_8O_{22}(OH)_2$

These two minerals form another

Hornblende crystal

series, like that between tremolite and actinolite. In this case, riebeckite is rich in iron while glaucophane is rich in magnesium. Well-developed, elongated crystals of these minerals, belonging to the monoclinic system, are rare, and fibrous masses usually occur. The hardness is 5–6 and the specific gravity increases from 3 to 3·4, according to the iron content. Glaucophane is grey to light blue, while riebeckite is dark blue to black. These translucent minerals have a vitreous lustre, but the fibrous forms are silky. Glaucophane is found in sodium-rich schists with chlorite, epidote, garnet, jadeite and muscovite. Riebeckite commonly occurs in igneous rocks. Veins of a fibrous variety, crocidolite or blue asbestos, occur in ironstones.

Hornblende $(Ca,Na)_{2-3}(Mg,Fe,Al)_5$ $(Si,Al)_8O_{22}(OH)_2$

Hornblende is the commonest amphibole. It occurs in many igneous and metamorphic rocks, being associated with garnet and quartz. Its hardness is 5–6 and the specific gravity is 3–3·5. The crystals have the symmetry of the monoclinic system. But hornblende also occurs in massive, granular and fibrous forms. This translucent to nearly opaque mineral ranges in colour from light green to dark green and black. The streak is white to grey and the lustre is vitreous.

91

Muscovite

Biotite

Clinoclore variety of
chlorite, with red garnets

Mica

Micas are a group of minerals, with perfect basal cleavage. One type, including muscovite, is rich in aluminium. The other type, including biotite, is rich in iron and magnesium. Micas often form blocks of thin flexible sheets. Transparent sheets of muscovite were used for windowpanes in Russia. Micas occur in many igneous and metamorphic rocks. Fragments are frequently found in sandstones and siltstones.

Muscovite $KAl_2(AlSi_3O_{10})(OH,F)_2$

Tabular, hexagonal crystals of muscovite, belonging to the monoclinic system, are rare. The mineral is usually found as scattered flakes or as blocks of thin, flexible sheets. The specific gravity is $2 \cdot 8 - 2 \cdot 9$ and the hardness is 2—3. This transparent to translucent mineral is mostly colourless to light grey, or green or brown. The lustre is vitreous to pearly.

Biotite $K(Mg,Fe)_3AlSi_3O_{10}(OH,F)_2$

The often tabular crystals of biotite belong to the monoclinic system. Biotite also occurs as scattered flakes or as blocks of thin sheets. This black, dark brown to greenish-black mineral is transparent to translucent. The specific gravity is $2 \cdot 7 - 3 \cdot 4$ and the hardness is 2—3. The lustre is vitreous to submetallic.

Chlorite
$(Mg,Fe,Al)_6(SiAl)_4O_{10}(OH)_8$

Chlorite is a group of minerals formed by the alteration of amphiboles, micas and pyroxenes. They are found in igneous, metamorphic and sedimentary rocks. The crystals belong to the monoclinic system. Chlorites also occur in scaly, massive and earthy forms. The specific gravity is $2 \cdot 6 - 2 \cdot 8$ and the hardness, 2—3. Chlorites have perfect basal cleavage. Although mostly green and translucent, chlorites may be yellow, brown or violet. The lustre is vitreous to earthy.

Serpentine $Mg_3Si_2O_5(OH)_4$

Serpentine, once thought to be a cure for snake bites, is another group of secondary minerals formed from altered olivines and pyroxenes in igneous rocks. The crystals, of the monoclinic system, have perfect basal cleavage. The variety chrysotile is fibrous and is one type of asbestos. Antigorite is a layered or platy variety. The specific gravity is $2 \cdot 5 - 2 \cdot 6$ and the hardness, $2\frac{1}{2}-4$. Serpentine is mostly green, but brown, grey, white and yellow types occur. This translucent to opaque mineral has a greasy lustre. Fibrous forms are silky and massive types are earthy.

Yellow serpentine (Norway)

Vermiculite $(Mg,Fe,Al)_3(Al,Si)_4O_{10}(OH)_2 . 4H_2O$

Vermiculite is another group of secondary minerals. The platy crystals, of the monoclinic system, have perfect basal cleavage. The specific gravity is $2 \cdot 3$ and the hardness, $1\frac{1}{2}$. Vermiculite is translucent, yellow or brown, with a pearly lustre.

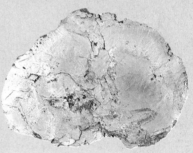

Vermiculite (West Indies)

Kaolinite $Al_2Si_2O_5(OH)_4$

Kaolinite is formed by the alteration of silicates rich in aluminium. The crystals have the symmetry of the triclinic system and perfect basal cleavage. But kaolinite usually occurs in dull, white earthy masses. The specific gravity is $2 \cdot 6 - 2 \cdot 7$ and the hardness is $2 - 2\frac{1}{2}$.

Kaolinite

Talc $Mg_3Si_4O_{10}(OH)_2$

Talc, used in talcum powder, is formed by the alteration of amphiboles, olivine and pyroxenes in metamorphic rocks. Crystals, of the monoclinic system, are rare. They have perfect basal cleavage. Talc usually occurs in granular and layered forms. Massive talc, called steatite or soapstone, has a soft, soapy feel. The specific gravity is $2 \cdot 6 - 2 \cdot 8$ and the hardness is 1. This translucent mineral may be white or grey to greenish, yellowish, reddish or brownish in colour.

Talc: steatite variety (North Carolina, USA)

93

Rock crystal

Citrine

Amethyst quartz

Silica Group

The silica group consists of those minerals with the basic formula SiO_2. Some of them, including quartz, are crystalline. Others, such as those in the chalcedony group (pages 96–7), are cryptocrystalline. This means that the crystals are so small that they can be seen only through a microscope. Agate (page 98) is a form of chalcedony. Opal (page 99) is chemically similar to quartz, but it is amorphous. This means that it has no regular crystal structure. Instead, it is composed of minute silica spheres, closely packed together.

Quartz SiO_2

Quartz, which is mostly pure silicon dioxide, is one of the commonest of all rock-forming minerals. It occurs in many igneous, metamorphic and sedimentary rocks, such as granite, gneiss and sandstone. It also forms nearly all of some rocks, including quartzite and some sandstones. Quartz also occurs in mineral veins, where it is associated with many metal ores. Some of the best-developed crystals of quartz come from vein deposits.

Other fine specimens occur in geodes in some sedimentary rocks. Besides sometimes being used in jewellery, quartz is also made into abrasives and used in the manufacture of glass. Pure forms are used in watches and telecommunications equipment, including radios.

The crystals of quartz have the symmetry of the trigonal system. They are usually six-sided and elongated. The crystals also often have parallel grooves running across them, at right angles to their length. Twinning is common. Quartz also occurs in massive forms. The hardness is 7, which distinguishes it from the much softer calcite crystals, which may look similar. On beaches, fragments of quartz often resemble bits of worn glass, but flint scratches glass, while it glides over quartz, leaving no mark.

Quartz has a specific gravity of 2·65. It has no cleavage and it fractures conchoidally (like the outside of a seashell). This transparent to translucent mineral has a vitreous lustre and a white streak. Pure quartz is colourless or white, but a wide range of colours occurs, caused by such factors as impurities and exposure to radioactive rays.

Rock crystal is a colourless variety of quartz used in jewellery and to make high-quality glass. Its name comes from the Greek *krystallos*, meaning ice. Some Greeks thought that it was a kind of ice, frozen so hard that it would not melt.

Citrine is a yellow, transparent variety, resembling topaz (page 86). The colour is probably caused by iron trioxide. Natural citrines are comparatively rare. Some amethysts turn yellow when they are heated to about 250°C (482°F) and such yellow stones may be used as gems instead of citrines.

Amethyst is a purple form of quartz, often used in jewellery. Its name comes from the Greek word, *amethystos*, meaning unintoxicated. People once wore amulets of amethyst to prevent them from getting drunk.

Smoky quartz is a smoky-brown variety. The colour is often caused by radiation from adjacent or included radioactive minerals. Black varieties are called morion.

Rose quartz is a rose-red or pink variety, caused possibly by the presence of manganese oxide. It is usually found in massive forms.

Milky quartz is a white, translucent to nearly opaque variety. It contains no impurities. The milky colour is caused by many microscopic flaws in the crystals which refract light.

Tiger's eye is a form of crocidolite (page 90) that has been partly replaced by silica. This yellow to brown mineral displays a chatoyant (cat's eye) effect when cut in a rounded shape.

Rose quartz

Smoky quartz

Milky-rose quartz

Tiger's eye

Chalcedony

Carnelian necklace

Chalcedony SiO_2

Chalcedony is a compact variety of silica, composed of minute crystals of quartz. It is slightly softer than quartz and it is denser than opal — minerals which are other forms of silicon dioxide. Chalcedony was named after Chalcedon, near Istanbul, Turkey. There are two main kinds of chalcedony: the mostly evenly-coloured varieties, and agates, which have various colours divided into bands or zones. Chalcedony was used in jewellery in ancient times by such people as the Babylonians, Persians, Greeks and Romans. A signet ring containing chalcedony was supposed to bring luck to the wearer during legal actions. The mineral was also a popular ornamental and gem stone in the Middle Ages. Today, however, it is probably less widely used, but it remains extremely popular with mineral collectors.

The crystals in chalcedony are so small that they can be viewed only through a microscope. The mineral is often found in masses of rounded lumps (botryoidal) or in stalactite-like forms. It may also be massive or it may occur as nodules. The specific gravity is $2 \cdot 6$ and the hardness is about $6\frac{1}{2}$. This transparent to subtranslucent mineral has a vitreous to waxy lustre. The colour ranges from white and grey to red, brown and black. The varieties used in ornaments and jewellery are those with distinctive colouring.

Carnelian is a red to reddish-brown variety, which has been coloured by iron oxides. It is translucent and this distinguishes it from jasper, which is red but opaque. Many carnelians now used in jewellery are not natural stones. Instead, they have been stained red artificially. Carnelian merges into another variety, which is called sard. Sard is light brown to dark brown. It is often impossible to draw a distinct line between carnelian and sard.

Jasper is a generally red, opaque

variety. It is often impure, containing some clay. It may also be brown, green, grey-blue or yellow in colour. Sometimes, the colours occur in bands or spots. Jasper is used in jewellery and often to decorate buildings, such as for interior fittings.

Chrysoprase is a beautiful apple-green variety of chalcedony. It was a popular ornamental stone in the Middle Ages. Another variety, called heliotrope, is green and covered by red spots. These spots resemble blood, which explains heliotrope's other name, bloodstone.

Chert, which may be white, brown or grey, and flint, which is dark brown to black, are other impure forms of chalcedony. These common translucent to opaque varieties are described and illustrated on page 117.

Chalcedony occurs in fissures and hollows in igneous and sedimentary rocks. It is often precipitated from hot water which contains dissolved silica. It occurs in veins and replaces dissolved cavities in various sedimentary rocks. Sometimes chalcedony replaces the remains of animals and plants, producing fossils of such things as shells and sponges. In Arizona, fossil tree trunks have been replaced by chalcedony, producing petrified wood.

Agate SiO_2

Agate has long been a popular mineral used in jewellery, especially for cameo brooches, and for such ornaments as ashtrays, boxes, goblets and paperweights. Agate is a form of chalcedony. It is characterized by the fine bands or zones of differing colours which permeate it. Samples may contain shades of black, blue, brown, green, grey, red or white. Agate is precipitated from water containing plenty of dissolved silica. It is often deposited in cavities in lava, and worn nodules or pebbles of agate may be found on beaches in some areas. When a nodule is split apart, the bands of colour are seen to form circular or irregularly

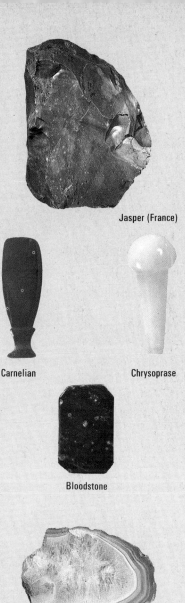

Jasper (France)

Carnelian

Chrysoprase

Bloodstone

Agate

97

Sardonyx

Onyx

Mocha stone

rounded patterns. Sometimes, quartz crystals occur at the centre. The differing colours are caused partly by slight changes in the chemicals present in the solution during the formation of agate.

Agate has a specific gravity of about 2·6 and a hardness of $6\frac{1}{2}$–7. It has no cleavage and it fractures conchoidally. There are several distinct varieties of agate.

Onyx is a variety which usually combines regular and straight bands of black and white. Sardonyx is a brownish-red variety of onyx. Moss agate is a translucent, milky-white, bluish-white or colourless variety. It contains impurities, which appear in the mineral as delicate, moss-like or branching lines, coloured black, brown or green. The impurities are most commonly a deposit of manganese oxide. Mocha stone is similar. It contains fern-like shapes.

Besides its uses in jewellery and in ornament-making, agate has various other uses, because it is a tough mineral. For example, it is used in tools, such as grinding apparatus. It is also used in instruments which require hard, long-wearing parts. For example, it is often used as the pivots in accurate balances.

Opal $SiO_2 . nH_2O$

Opal has been a precious and prized gemstone for the last 2500 years. It is particularly noted for its brilliant iridescence, or opalescence, causing it to display rainbow colours as it is rotated. Iridescence occurs because light is split up by the internal structure of the mineral. Opal was once thought to bring good luck. But, in recent times, some people have considered it to be unlucky. Besides its importance in jewellery, opal is used to make abrasives. It is also made into products which are used for insulation.

This hydrous, amorphous mineral usually contains up to about one-tenth water. But water may form as much as one-third of some samples. Like agate, opal is formed by precipitation from water (at fairly low temperatures).

Opal fills fissures and cavities in igneous and sedimentary rocks. It is especially common around hot springs and geysers. It may also be formed by the chemical weathering and decomposition of rocks. Opal forms the skeletons of some tiny organisms that live in water. A rock, diatomite, is composed largely of these skeletons, which pile up in ponds and lakes.

The mineral opal is found in masses or in small veins. It may be botryoidal or stalactite-like in character. The specific gravity ranges from 1·8 to 2·3 and the hardness is $5\frac{1}{2}$–$6\frac{1}{2}$. It has no cleavage and it fractures conchoidally. This transparent to translucent mineral has a vitreous to resinous lustre, although it may sometimes be pearly. Colours vary considerably from colourless and milky-white to grey, red, brown, blue and green to nearly black. Some varieties of opal are described below.

The so-called precious opal may be milky-white or tinged with yellow. It is brilliantly iridescent. Black opal, a variety of precious opal, is also iridescent. It is the most valuable of all varieties. It once cost more than diamond.

Common opal is translucent and may be one of several colours. However, it lacks iridescence.

Fire opal is transparent. It may be red or yellow in colour. Fire opal, as its name suggests, displays a fiery play of colours. Hyalite, or glassy opal, is generally colourless. This attractive variety may be botryoidal or stalactite-like in form. Wood opal is wood which has been replaced by opal. Liver opal, which is also called menilite, is grey or brown. It is often found in rounded or flattened concretions, which are much like flint.

One particularly interesting variety of opal is hydrophane. This light-coloured, rather dull mineral loses its water and its iridescence when it is exposed to the air. However, the iridescence returns when the sample is placed in water.

Kinds of opal

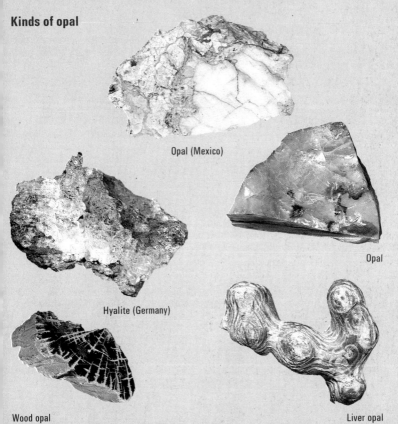

Opal (Mexico)

Opal

Hyalite (Germany)

Wood opal

Liver opal

Orthoclase

Plagioclase : Labradorite (Canada)

Microline : Amazonstone variety (Colorado, USA)

Lapis lazuli (Torquay, England)

Feldspars, Feldspathoids

Feldspars, the most abundant of all rock-forming mineral groups, are found in igneous, metamorphic and sedimentary rocks. Feldspars are aluminium silicates, which also contain one or more of the following elements: barium, calcium, potassium or sodium. Feldspars include orthoclase, microline and the plagioclase series.

Feldspathoids, such as lazurite, contain the same elements, but usually have much less silicon.

Orthoclase, Microline $KAlSi_3O_8$

These two abundant feldspars are very similar. They occur in igneous and metamorphic rocks and, as grains, in sedimentary rocks.

The hardness of both minerals is $6-6\frac{1}{2}$ and the specific gravity is $2.5-2.6$. Orthoclase crystals belong to the monoclinic system, while microline belongs to the triclinic system. But it is often hard to tell the crystals apart. Both have two good cleavages. Orthoclase is white to pink and sometimes red. Microline is similar, but the bright green variety, amazonstone, is

easy to recognize. These translucent to subtranslucent minerals have a vitreous lustre.

Plagioclase Feldspars
$NaAlSi_3O_8 - CaAl_2Si_2O_8$

Plagioclase feldspars form a series of minerals in which the amount of sodium and calcium varies. One type, illustrated above, is labradorite. It contains more calcium than sodium. These minerals occur widely in many igneous and some metamorphic rocks. Grains occur in sedimentary rocks.

The crystals, of the triclinic system, are usually column-like or tabular. They have two good cleavages. The lustre is vitreous. But cleavage surfaces are pearly and those of labradorite often show a play of blues and greens. These minerals also occur in massive and granular forms. The hardness is $6-6\frac{1}{2}$. The specific gravity is $2.6-2.8$. These transparent to translucent minerals are often white. Pink, green and brown types also occur.

Lazurite
$(Na,Ca)_8(Al,Si)_{12}O_{24}(S,SO_4)$
Lazurite, a deep blue, translucent mineral occurs in the rock lapis-lazuli, with calcite and pyrite. Lapis-lazuli is used in jewellery. Lazurite crystals, of the cubic system, are rare and the mineral is usually massive. The hardness is $5-5\frac{1}{2}$ and the specific gravity, $2\cdot4$. The fracture is uneven and the lustre is vitreous.

Zeolites
Zeolites are secondary minerals, formed when feldspars and other aluminium-rich minerals are altered. Water is chemically combined in zeolites. Zeolites are unusual in that, when they lose or re-absorb water, their internal structures and crystal forms are unchanged. Zeolites include analcite, chabazite, stilbite and natrolite.

Analcite $NaAlSi_2O_6.H_2O$
Analcite (or analcime) occurs in cavities in basaltic and sedimentary rocks. The crystal system is cubic, but analcite also occurs in massive forms. The hardness is $5\frac{1}{2}$ and the specific gravity

is $2\cdot2-2\cdot3$. This transparent to translucent mineral is usually colourless, white or grey, but it may be greenish, pinkish or yellowish.

Chabazite $CaAl_2Si_4O_{12}.6H_2O$
Chabazite occurs in cavities in basalts. Its crystals belong to the trigonal system. The hardness is $4\frac{1}{2}$ and the specific gravity is $2-2\cdot2$. It is usually white or yellow, but it may be pinkish or red. It is transparent to translucent and has a vitreous lustre.

Stilbite $NaCa_2(Al_5Si_{13})O_{36}.14H_2O$
Stilbite also occurs in cavities in basalt. The crystals, of the monoclinic system, often form in sheaf-like groups. Stilbite may also be massive or globular. The hardness is $3\frac{1}{2}-4$ and the specific gravity is $2\cdot1-2\cdot2$. This transparent to translucent mineral is white and, sometimes, yellowish, pink or red.

Natrolite $Na_2Al_2Si_3O_{10}.2H_2O$
Natrolite, a common zeolite, is found in cavities in igneous rocks. This colourless or white, transparent to translucent mineral belongs to the orthorhombic crystal system. The crystals are often needle-like and arranged in radiating clusters. Natrolite also occurs in compact masses. The hardness is 5 and the specific gravity is $2\cdot2-2\cdot3$. The lustre is vitreous.

Analcite

Chabazite (Canada)

Stilbite (Pennsylvania, USA)

Guide to Rocks

In this Guide, igneous rocks are described on pages 102–9; sedimentary rocks on pages 110–9; and metamorphic rocks on pages 120–1. Tektites, meteorites and Moon rocks are covered on pages 122–3.

Igneous Rocks

Intrusive igneous rocks are described on pages 103–5 and extrusive igneous rocks on pages 106–9.

Certain features of igneous rocks help us to identify them. Some important features, including grain size, texture and structure, are discussed on pages 46–9, with explanations of some of the technical terms used to describe igneous rocks.

Classifying Igneous Rocks

Although magma is a highly complex substance, igneous rocks are formed largely from only a few *essential*, or *rock-forming* minerals. The essential minerals are all silicates: orthoclase and plagioclase feldspars, micas, amphiboles, pyroxenes, olivines and quartz. Together, these minerals make up more than 90 per cent of all igneous rocks. Other *accessory*, or *non-essential* minerals also occur, but in small amounts.

Four main kinds of igneous rocks are classified according to their silica content. They are acid igneous rocks (over 66 per cent silica), intermediate rocks (52–66 per cent silica), basic rocks (45–52 per cent silica) and ultrabasic rocks (less than 45 per cent silica). *Acid* igneous rocks often con-

Scandinavian granite

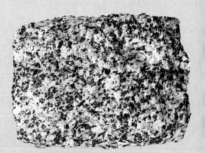

Hornblende granite

Porphyritic granite with orthoclase phenocrysts

Granodiorite

Graphic granite

Pegmatite with mica phenocrysts

tain a high proportion of orthoclase feldspars (page 100) and quartz (pages 94–5). These rocks are mostly light in colour. *Intermediate* igneous rocks contain less quartz and sometimes plagioclase feldspars partly replace orthoclase. *Basic* igneous rocks are darker. They contain little or no quartz, and augite (a pyroxene, page 88) and plagioclase feldspar (page 100) predominate. *Ultrabasic* igneous rocks are rich in ferromagnesian minerals, such as olivine (page 82) and some pyroxenes (page 88). Ultrabasic rocks contain no quartz and little or no feldspar. They are mostly dark in colour.

Granite, Granodiorite

Granites and granodiorites are related rocks. Together, they are the commonest of all intrusive igneous rocks. Granite is a popular building and ornamental stone. However, the term granite is sometimes wrongly used for other hard rocks. For example, a rock called *petit granit* in Belgium is really a limestone.

Geologically, granite is an acid igneous rock. The essential minerals are orthoclase feldspar, quartz (usually 20–40 per cent), and often some mica (muscovite or biotite). Plagioclase feldspar may also occur, especially in varieties that grade into granodiorite, a granite in which plagioclase

feldspars are more abundant than orthoclase feldspars. Some granites contain hornblende or tourmaline, while apatite, magnetite, sphene and zircon are accessory minerals.

Granite is usually mottled. Shades of white, grey, pink or red are common. Granodiorite is usually coloured in shades of grey. Both rocks are coarse to very coarse-grained, because the magma cooled slowly far below the surface. Granite may be granular or porphyritic, in which case, the phenocrysts (large crystals) are feldspar. One of the types illustrated on page 102 has orthoclase phenocrysts. Some granites also contain xenoliths.

Granites occur in almost all kinds of intrusive structures. In some places, they may be metamorphic in origin. Granite may decompose into clay minerals, such as kaolin. But it may resist weathering and erosion, and form rugged landscapes.

Pegmatites

Pegmatites are extremely coarse-grained intrusive igneous rocks, related to granite. They may contain crystals which are several centimetres (or even metres) across. The chief minerals in pegmatites are orthoclase feldspars, quartz and muscovite, and so pegmatites are acid igneous rocks.

They form after most of a mass of magma has solidified into granite.

The remaining molten material, which is rich in a large number of accessory minerals, is intruded into veins or dykes, usually towards the edge of the granite mass, or in the rocks surrounding it. Besides those found in granite, other accessory minerals in pegmatites include beryl, chalcopyrite, corundum, fluorite, galena, pyrite, rutile, spodumene and topaz. Pegmatites are often mined for a wide range of mineral ores and rare elements. They are also excellent places to look for fine mineral specimens.

Pegmatites occur in the same colours as granite. One variety, called graphic granite, has large feldspar crystals intergrown with elongated, angular quartz grains. This rock has patterns resembling Hebrew and other ancient writing.

Syenite

Syenite is a coarse-grained, intermediate igneous rock. It is similar to granite, but it is much less common. Also, syenite contains little or no quartz, although the quartz syenite variety has up to 10 per cent of that mineral. Accessory minerals include aegirine, apatite, augite, biotite, hornblende, sphene and zircon. This intrusive, red, pink, white or grey rock occurs in stocks (small batholiths), sills and dykes. It is commonly granular and it sometimes has a porphyritic texture.

Diorite

Diorite is a coarse-grained, intrusive, intermediate igneous rock, composed essentially of plagioclase feldspar and hornblende. It may also contain biotite and/or a pyroxene, with apatite, iron oxides and sphene as accessory minerals. Diorite usually has an even texture, but porphyritic textures and samples containing xenoliths are also found. Diorite is usually black and white, but shades of green and pink are found. This rock occurs in stocks and dykes.

Gabbro

Gabbro is a coarse-grained, basic igneous rock. It is composed of light-coloured plagioclase feldspar, together with such dark minerals as augite and olivine. Accessory minerals found in gabbro include biotite, chromite, hornblende, magnetite, quartz and serpentine. Gabbro forms from the same kind of magma which solidifies on the surface as basalt, but gabbro is an intrusive rock, found in large intrusions, stocks, sills and dykes. This grey to black rock is often layered, with light and dark bands. It is usually granular.

Serpentinite

Serpentinite is a rock composed mostly of serpentine (see page 92), with hornblende, iron oxides, mica and sometimes garnet as accessory minerals. It is probably an ultrabasic, olivine-rich rock, such as peridotite, which has been altered, and so it is really a secondary rock. It is popular as an ornamental and building stone, because of its attractive colouring. Serpentinite commonly occurs in shades of green to black. But it may be streaked or mottled with black, white, green and red. This medium to coarse-grained and often banded rock occurs in large masses in stocks. It is also sometimes found in folded metamorphic rocks.

Diabase

Diabase, also called dolerite, is a medium-grained, basic igneous rock, found in dykes and sills. Colours range from black to grey or green, but some specimens are black and white. Diabase is composed of olivine, with a pyroxene or plagioclase feldspar. Accessory minerals include biotite, hornblende and quartz. Samples of diabase may be pitted with vesicles. These vesicles are sometimes filled with other minerals, giving the rock an amygdaloidal texture. The rock may also have a porphyritic texture.

Syenite
(Germany)

Gabbro

Diorite

Serpentinite with stichtite, a
hydrated magnesium chrome-
carbonate (Tasmania, Australia)

Diabase
(Cumbria, England)

Extrusive Igneous Rocks

Extrusive igneous rocks are of two main kinds: those formed from streams of molten lava; and pyroclastic rocks, which are ejected from volcanoes (see pages 108–9 for examples).

According to their appearance, there are three main kinds of lava. Ropy lava, also called *pahoehoe* (a Hawaiian word meaning rough or spiny), is illustrated on this page. It was erupted from Mt Vesuvius, the great volcano which overlooks the Bay of Naples in Italy. The second kind of lava is rough block lava, also called *aa* (Hawaiian for satiny). Finally, pillow lava forms when lava is erupted under the sea or when lava flows enter water. Pillow lava resembles sack-shaped piles of rock. The surface is usually extremely fine-grained or even glassy. This texture is caused by fast cooling. Inside, however, the texture is usually more granular.

The more fluid lavas, which may pour downhill at considerable speeds and for great distances, solidify into basic igneous rocks, such as basalt. Basalt is, by far, the commonest extrusive igneous rock formed from lava. On the other hand, acid magmas are stiff and sluggish. They form such rocks as rhyolite. Trachyte and andesite are intermediate igneous rocks formed from lava.

Basalt

This fine-grained to glassy basic igneous rock is usually solidified lava, although some basalts may form near the surface in small dykes and sills. Basalt has built up many volcanoes and oceanic islands, such as Hawaii. It covers some vast areas. About 700,000 cubic kilometres (168,000 cubic miles) of basalt is piled up on the Deccan plateau of India. Sometimes, cooling basalt becomes jointed, breaking into hexagonal columns, such as at the Giant's Causeway, Northern Ireland (see picture on page 48).

Chemically, basalt is similar to gabbro. It is composed of plagioclase

Ropy lava
(Vesuvius, 1858)

Basalt (Northern Ireland)

Vesicular basalt

Rhyolite

Trachyte

feldspar, olivine and a pyroxene, usually augite, together with some accessory minerals. But, often, none of the minerals are identifiable, except under a microscope. This black to dark grey rock may, when it is exposed to the air, acquire a reddish or greenish crust. It is often vesicular or amygdaloidal, when the vesicles are filled with such minerals as calcite, chalcedony or zeolites. Basalt is sometimes porphyritic and xenoliths are not uncommon.

Rhyolite

This fine-grained acid igneous rock is similar to granite, but the crystals cannot usually be identified by the naked eye. However, phenocrysts of quartz, feldspar, hornblende or mica sometimes occur. Rhyolite often shows flow banding. Vesicles and amygdales also occur. The colours are varied, including grey, white, greenish, reddish and brownish. The magma from which rhyolite forms is very stiff and flows only short distances before hardening. Often, it forms plugs in the vents of volcanoes.

Trachyte

Trachyte is a fine-grained intermediate igneous rock. It is usually grey, but may be white or pink. Chemically, it is similar to syenite. It is composed of

Pyroxene andesite
(Cumbria, England)

orthoclase feldspar, some quartz (less than 10 per cent), with small amounts of dark minerals, such as aegirine, augite, biotite or hornblende. It is usually porphyritic and forms mainly from lava flows.

Andesite

Named after the Andes Mountains, this fine-grained to glassy intermediate igneous rock is confined to volcanoes on continental land masses, notably in areas where mountain building is in progress. It is the second most abundant extrusive igneous rock.

Chemically, andesite is similar to diorite. Colours range from grey, purple,

107

Pitchstone (Scotland)

Obsidian

Pumice breccia

brown and green to almost black. It is often porphyritic, in which case, the phenocrysts of plagioclase feldspar, biotite, hornblende or augite may be identified. It can also be vesicular or amygdaloidal.

Pitchstone, Obsidian

These two acid igneous rocks are both glassy, the result of rapid cooling of magma. They occur in solidified lava, and also in small dykes and sills. They are black, brown or grey in colour but, while obsidian is shiny, pitchstone is dullish and resinous-looking. Chemically, they have the same composition as rhyolite.

Phenocrysts are rare in obsidian, but feldspar and quartz phenocrysts are fairly common in pitchstone. Both rocks may be flow-banded or spotted. Obsidian has a conchoidal (shell-like) fracture. The edges of shattered fragments of obsidian have sharp edges and Stone Age people used such fragments to make tools and weapons.

Pumice

Pumice forms from frothy acid lava, which contains masses of bubbles of gas. Following extremely rapid cooling, this frothy lava solidifies into a porous and glassy rock with a honey-combed structure. It is usually grey and, sometimes, yellowish in colour. Pumice is ejected during volcanic eruptions, especially those that occur in the sea or near water. After eruptions, sailors have seen large rafts of pumice floating on the sea.

Pumice is sometimes used as an abrasive and small pieces were once used in many homes for removing stains from the hands. Pumice, mixed with cement, makes a useful, lightweight building material. The picture on this page shows pumice breccia, a mass of angular fragments.

Volcanic Bombs

Volcanic bombs are lumps of liquid lava which are ejected from volcanoes during eruptions. As they fly through the air, the lumps of lava are hardened and shaped. Their glassy crusts often crack, resembling bread crust. Most bombs are shaped like globes, spheres or spindles, but some are more irregular. Geologists use the term bomb for fragments which are more than 3·2 centimetres (1·26 inches) long. But some are very large. An accumulation of bombs and other smaller fragments form rocks called agglomerates or volcanic breccia.

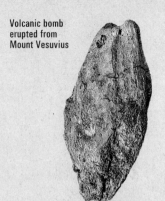
Volcanic bomb erupted from Mount Vesuvius

Ignimbrite

This igneous rock consists of small pieces of ash set in a mass of fine fragments of volcanic glass. Ignimbrite is formed by *nuées ardentes*, (a French term meaning 'glowing clouds'), which are erupted from some volcanoes. These clouds contain extremely hot gas and ash. From the volcano's vent, they flow quickly downhill in the direction of the wind, burning everything in their paths. When the fragments settle, they are still so hot that they become welded together to form a hard, compact rock. One famous *nuée ardente* from the volcano, Mt Pelée, destroyed the city of St Pierre, capital of Martinique, in 1902. Some 30,000 people perished.

Ignimbrite (Tenerife)

Tuff

Tuff is a fine-grained pyroclastic rock, composed mainly of volcanic ash. The grains of ash are mostly less than 2 millimetres (0·08 inches) across. Pyroclastic rocks with larger grains are usually called agglomerates or volcanic breccias. But some tuff contains lapilli, which are stones between the size of a pea and a walnut. Tuff may also contain fine glassy fragments and mineral crystals. Following an eruption, fine grains of ash may be exploded high into the air, where winds may carry them hundreds of kilometres before they finally fall. Tuffs are often layered and fine-grained varieties may resemble sedimentary rocks.

Tuff (Salop, England)

Conglomerate
(Puddingstone)

Tillite

Sedimentary Rocks

Sedimentary rocks are the commonest rocks on the Earth's surface, because they cover about three-quarters of the world's land areas.

They are of three main kinds: clastic rocks (composed of fragments of worn rocks and usually cemented together by minerals precipitated from water); chemical sedimentary rocks, which were formed by chemical action; and organic rocks, which consist mostly of once-living matter. The origin, nature and classification of sedimentary rocks are described on pages 50–5, in the first part of this book.

In this Guide, clastic sedimentary rocks are described on pages 110–3. They range from coarse-grained conglomerates and breccias to fine-grained mudstones and shales. Limestones, which all consist mostly of calcite, but which may be clastic, chemical or organic in origin, are described on pages 114–5. Some other important chemical sedimentary rocks are covered on pages 116–7, while other organic rocks, notably kinds of coal, are described on pages 118–9.

Conglomerates

Conglomerates, sometimes called puddingstones, are coarse-grained (rudaceous) rocks. They contain rounded pebbles (gravel or shingle), set in fine or medium-grained silt or sand (called the matrix). They are often cemented by calcite or silica.

The pebbles may be almost any kind of hard rock, including quartzite, quartz, chert, and so on. As a result, the colour is very variable. Conglomerates form in such places as lake and sea beaches and in river beds. The pebbles have been rounded by constant rubbing, which occurs either during transportation or on beaches, where seawater moves them around. These rocks do not usually show bedding. Fossils are rare.

Breccia

Breccias are composed of the same kinds of large fragments, matrix and cements as conglomerates. The difference is that the larger fragments are angular, not rounded. This means that they have not been moved far from their point of origin. Breccia may form from scree or from shattered rocks at the base of a cliff.

Tillite

Tillites are rocks formed from till, or boulder clay, a substance transported and deposited by bodies of ice, glaciers and ice sheets. Till contains grains of many sizes, including extremely fine 'rock flour', stones and even boulders. Compact till, or tillite, is usually dark grey to greenish black in colour. It is often bedded, each bed representing a new glacial deposit. Tillite often rests on a smooth, ice-worn surface. The presence of tillite proves that the area was once glaciated. It is widely distributed in parts of northern Europe and northern North America in areas that were buried under ice sheets during the last Ice Age. The alternative name for tillite, boulder clay, describes well the uneven texture of this rock.

Sandstone

Sandstone is a common, medium-grained (arenaceous) rock. It is porous, that is, it has pores which can be filled with water. Sandstone usually forms in water, but some are ancient sands, which have piled up on land in dry regions. Desert sandstones are usually red, such as the Devonian sandstone shown on this page. (The Devonian is a period in Earth history, which lasted from 395 to 345 million years ago). Desert sandstones may be cross-bedded. This means that the beds, or layers, are not parallel to one another. Instead, they are tilted and, in an exposed cliff, one series of layers

often appears at an angle to other series of layers above and below it. Cross-bedding is shown in the photograph of sandstone on page 54. It may have resulted from sand dunes advancing over and burying one another. Other sandstones may be brown, green, yellow, grey or white. Green-sands are sandstones coloured by glauconite, a mica mineral.

Grains of the tough mineral quartz are the chief components of sandstones, but feldspar, micas and other minerals may also occur. Sandstones are sometimes classified according to the cementing material which binds the grains together. Sandstones cemented by calcite are calcareous sandstones; those cemented by iron oxides are ferruginous sandstones; and those cemented by silica are siliceous sandstones.

The grains in sandstones are usually rounded. If they are angular, then the rock is often called a grit. Sandstones are commonly bedded and they contain fossils.

Arkose, Greywacke

Arkose and greywacke are two sandstones, formed in different ways. Arkose is a red, pink or grey rock, which contains a high proportion of feldspar

Breccia in New
Red Sandstone

Devonian sandstone

Arkose

Greywacke

(usually between 25 and 50 per cent). Most of the rest is quartz, although mica minerals may also occur. Arkose forms from granite. It contains angular grains, showing that it formed possibly in alluvial fans, or on flood plains, near granite outcrops. Arkose is often bedded, but fossils are rare. This rock may resemble granite, but the grains are fragmented and not closely interlocked as they are in granite.

Greywacke is a poorly-sorted sandstone, with angular grains set in a finer matrix. Fossils are rare in this often massive rock. Geologists think that greywacke was formed in deep water beyond the continental shelf. The grains were swept there by fast-flowing underwater currents, called turbidity currents. These swift currents carry grains of assorted sizes far out to sea.

Siltstone

This fine-grained (argillaceous) rock consists of grains that are finer than sand, but coarser than clay. It is formed from silt, which usually piles up in beds on the floors of seas and lakes. The bedding is often very fine, as can be seen in the photograph on this page. Siltstone may be pale grey to black, or brown, buff or yellow in colour. The individual grains are usually just large enough to see. But it is not generally possible to recognize any individual minerals, except through a microscope. However, sometimes, tiny flakes of glittering mica and larger grains of feldspar and quartz can be identified. Nodules and concretions of various minerals may be found in siltstone. Fossils are often abundant and ripple marks may be seen on bedding planes.

Siltstone
(Salop, England)

Mudstone

Shale

Loess

Mudstone, Shale

These two rocks are formed from clay deposits that have been compressed and compacted so that the water is removed. They are similar in that they are both extremely fine-grained. The particles measure less than $\frac{1}{256}$ millimetre (0·0002 inches) across. However, mudstones, which are also called claystones, are generally un-layered and massive in form, while shale is finely-bedded. Shale will readily split into thin, flat sheets parallel to the bedding.

These rocks, which are smooth to the touch, are formed mostly from clay minerals. These minerals, including kaolinite, are complex silicates that result from the chemical weathering of such minerals as feldspars and micas. Besides clay minerals, there may also be tiny grains of calcite, feldspar, mica and quartz. Sometimes, pyrite crystals occur and pyrite may replace some fossils. If you find a pyrite fossil, remember that it will disintegrate after it has been exposed to the air. Such fossils can be preserved if treated chemically and coated with a sealing agent.

Both mudstone and shale occur in a wide variety of colours. Black types are usually coloured by carbonaceous matter, while iron oxides colour others brown or red. But these rocks may also be blue, dark green, grey or white. These rocks often form in the deeper parts of lakes and seas, and they are often rich in fossils. Sometimes, the bedding planes represent the surfaces of ancient mud flats, and they may be marked with the fossilized footprints of prehistoric animals, sun cracks, or with pits made by raindrops that fell long ago.

Loess

Loess is also called Aeolian clay. The word Aeolian comes from *Aiolos*, the Greek god of the winds, because loess is a fine silt or dust which has been transported and deposited by the wind, although it may, originally, have been of glacial origin. Thick strata of loess are found in parts of central Europe, the central United States and in northern China. Loess is eroded easily by rain and rivers. In China, where the loess is mostly yellow, it has coloured the waters of rivers, including the Yellow River (Hwang Ho), and the Yellow Sea. Loess may also be brown, buff or grey. Exposed loess cliffs often have many small tubes running down them. These tubes were probably made by plant roots. Mixed with humus, which consists of the decayed remains of plant and animal matter, loess forms rich soils, such as the fertile black earths of Russia.

113

Shelly limestone
(Dorset, England)

Limestones

Limestones are common, but very varied sedimentary rocks, which are made up mostly of the mineral calcite. Pure limestone is white, grey, cream, or yellow. But some are stained black, brown or red. In texture, limestones range from coarse to fine-grained, and they may be clastic, chemical or organic. For example, limestone breccias are composed of angular fragments. Chemical limestones are precipitated from water. They include oolitic limestone and travertine (page 116). Organic limestones consist of the remains of animals and plants.

Limestones are usually bedded, but the strata are not always clear. They often contain nodules of chert, flint and, sometimes, pyrite. Limestone is similar to another rock, dolomite. But if you put a drop of cold hydrochloric acid on limestone, it will effervesce. This reaction does not occur on dolomite.

Fossil Limestone

Some limestones are rich in fossils and so they are partly-organic rocks, such as the shelly limestone on this page. Some consist almost entirely of the remains of very small sea organisms.

Thick layers of limestone are built up in warm shallow seas from coral reefs and colonies of algae (plants, some of which secrete calcite). Coral limestones have been forming since the Ordovician period, which began about 500 million years ago. Another shallow-water organic limestone consists mostly of the skeletons and shells of bottom-living sea animals. A third, deep-sea deposit is made up of the remains of tiny, floating organisms.

Fossiliferous limestone
(Wenlock, England)

Oolitic Limestone

The word oolitic comes from two Greek words meaning *egg-stone*, and oolitic limestone resembles fish roe. It consists of masses of rounded grains of calcite, called ooliths, about 1 mm

Oolitic limestone
(Cotswold Hills, England)

(0·04 inches) across. Limestones called pisolites are similar, but the grains, or pisoliths, are larger, often the size of peas. Ooliths and pisoliths form when calcite is precipitated from seawater around grains of sand or shell, which roll over the sea floor. The rock is usually yellow to white, but it may be brown or red. Fossil fragments occur.

Chalk

Chalk is one of the purest forms of limestone and this mostly white or grey rock accumulated in clear water. It consists of coccoliths, which are very small calcareous plates of planktonic algae, and the remains of foraminifera. Fossils of larger animals also occur in chalk, as do nodules of flint and pyrite. Many chalk strata were formed in the Cretaceous period, between 141 and 65 million years ago. (*Creta* is the Latin name for chalk.) Chalk is forming today in parts of the oceans. Note that blackboard chalk is a form of gypsum and French chalk is talc.

Lime Mudstone

Lime or calcareous mudstone is a fine-grained, white, grey or yellow rock. It probably formed in deep parts of the oceans, partly from the remains of sea animals, and partly from precipitation. Fossils are rare. They were probably destroyed during the formation of the rock.

Dolomite

Dolomite, or magnesian limestone, consists mostly of the mineral dolomite (page 77). Most dolomites are secondary rocks, probably formed when water, containing magnesium, seeped through layers of limestone, replacing the calcite with dolomite. Recrystallization probably destroyed most of the fossils. The texture of dolomite is very variable and the beds are often thick and highly jointed. This white, cream or grey rock weathers to brown or pink.

Chalk (south-east England)

Calcareous mudstone (Somerset, England)

Dolomitic limestone

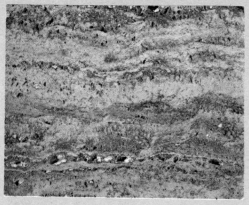
Travertine

Ironstone

Travertine

Travertine is composed chiefly of calcite and may be white, cream or yellow in colour. But impurities, such as iron oxides, may stain it red or brown. Sometimes, it contains bands of varying colours, and travertine is often used as an ornamental stone for fittings in buildings. Travertine is precipitated from calcite-rich water around springs in limestone areas and around hot springs and geysers in volcanic areas. It is a fairly compact rock, which distinguishes it from similar calc tufa, which is often pitted with masses of holes.

Rock salt (Poland)

Ironstone

Ironstones are sedimentary rocks, which are important commercially, because iron makes up at least 15 per cent of the rock. Iron minerals found in ironstones include siderite, hematite, magnetite, pyrite, and so on. Geologists think that ironstones were formed by the precipitation of iron from water seeping through existing strata, including mudstones, limestones and shales. They may be brown, green, red or yellow. The textures range from fine to coarse-grained and iron nodules may occur. Fossils are sometimes found in ironstones.

Rock Salt

Rock salt consists mostly of the mineral halite. It is an evaporite which forms when salty lakes, lagoons and enclosed seas dry up. As the water evaporates, thick beds of rock salt are formed. The rock may be crystalline or massive and it is mostly colourless. But it may be stained orange, red or yellow by impurities. Layers of rock salt are sometimes later distorted by pressure from overlying rocks. The rock salt may be compressed so that it flows upwards, intruding into the overlying rocks as a salt plug. The tops of salt plugs may trap oil and natural gas. Fossils are rare.

Rock gypsum

Rock gypsum is often formed in the same way as rock salt. But it may also be created when water is chemically combined with the mineral anhydrite (see pages 78–9). Rock gypsum may be brown, green, pink, red or white in colour. It often occurs between beds of sandstones and mudstones. The texture is variable and it may occur in massive, fibrous, sugary or earthy forms. Sometimes, large crystals are found in rock gypsum deposits.

Flint, Chert

Flint and chert are forms of the silicate mineral chalcedony. Hence, they are cryptocrystalline, containing crystals which are so small that they can be seen only through a microscope. Nodules of flint and chert are found in limestones, especially in chalk. They may be precipitated as secondary minerals in cavities in limestones. They sometimes form around fossils and, when you split a nodule apart, there may be a fossil inside. But chert also occurs in large beds. These are probably primary deposits from seawater on the sea bed.

Colours are varied. Flint is usually black or grey. But, when the outside of a nodule is weathered, it becomes coated with a whitish powder. Flint fractures conchoidally (like a sea shell) and the fresh edges are sharp. As a result, flint was used for tools and weapons by Stone Age people. Chert is a variety of flint with a flat, not a conchoidal, fracture.

Pyrite Nodules

Nodules of pyrite, a sulphide mineral, occur in limestones, shales, siltstones and other rocks. These nodules may be round, cylindrical or botryoidal in form. The outside of a nodule may be black, brown or yellow. But, inside, it is bronzy-yellow. It often consists of a mass of needle-like crystals, which radiate outwards from the centre, which may contain a nucleus around which the nodule formed.

Rock gypsum

Pyrite nodule

Flint from chalk

Banded chert

117

Coal

When plants and animals die, the once-living matter is decomposed by bacteria and other things. Eventually, the matter is converted into water, carbon dioxide and simple, inorganic salts. But, sometimes, the process of decay is halted. For example, this occurs in swamps or bogs, where rotting plant material is quickly buried. Fast burial protects it from oxygen, which is necessary for the complete breakdown of the material. Layers of partly rotted and buried plant matter become compacted into carbonaceous rocks, which are composed mostly of organic (once-living) carbon.

The first stage in this process can be studied today in the formation of peat on poorly-drained moorlands, marshes and shallow lakes.

Peat

Peat is a porous, light brown substance. Its plant character is clear, especially in the top layers. However, in thick deposits, the peat at the bottom is more compact and darker in colour. When peat is extracted, up to 90 per cent of its weight may be water. But when the peat is dried, it contains up to 60 per cent carbon.

Lignite

Lignite, or brown coal, represents the next stage in the formation of coal. This brown or black substance is much more compact than peat, but its organic origin is still apparent. When extracted, up to 50 per cent of its weight may be water. But, when the water has been removed, carbon accounts for 60 to 75 per cent of its dry weight. The world's main lignite deposits were formed mostly in the last 200 million years, whereas most of the world's bituminous coal and anthracite are much more ancient in origin. Lignite is mined as a fuel and also for the chemical industry.

Peat

Lignite (Greece)

Bituminous coal (Wales)

Anthracite (Wales)

Jet (Spain)

Oil shale (Scotland)

Bituminous Coal

Bituminous coal has various names, according to its uses. These names include household coal, coking coal, gas coal, steam coal, and so on. This hard, brittle substance contains up to 90 per cent carbon and it is a more efficient fuel than either peat or lignite. Evidence of its origin occurs occasionally in the form of plant fossils, such as the imprints of leaves.

Anthracite

Anthracite, which represents the final stage in coal formation, contains 95 per cent carbon. This shiny, black, structureless rock is clean to handle. It breaks with a conchoidal (shell-like) fracture. Geologists believe that, in addition to compaction, anthracite may also have been subject to pressure from Earth movements, and heat.

Most of the bituminous coal and anthracite mined today was formed in the Upper Carboniferous period, more than 280 million years ago. (This period is called the Pennsylvanian period in the United States.) At that time, luxuriant forests, including huge trees, giant ferns, mosses and horsetails, grew in vast swamps. An artist's impression of what these forests looked like is on page 54. Many of the coal seams formed during this period are not especially thick and they are separated by other strata, such as sandstones and mudstones. These inorganic rocks were formed when water covered the land and plant growth ceased for a while.

Jet

Jet is a black, fine-grained variety of coal which can be cut and shaped into jewellery and other decorative objects. Jet is either black lignite or cannel coal, a variety formed mostly from plant seeds, spores, algae and fungal material. Jet was widely used for jewellery in Britain when people went into mourning after the death of Prince Albert, Queen Victoria's husband, in 1861.

Oil Shale

Petroleum (or oil) and natural gas are other fossil fuels formed from once-living sea organisms whose remains were also buried rapidly. However, the oil and gas do not stay in the same place where they were buried. Instead, because they are light, they flow up through permeable rocks until they are trapped beneath a solid, impermeable layer. There, particles of oil and gas accumulate in quantities.

However, oil shale is a fine-grained sedimentary rock, which yields oil. Oil shale is black or dark grey, and it is found in association with coal strata. It contains a solid organic material called kerogen. When heated, kerogen yields a vapour from which oil can be extracted. The yield is low, about 20–40 litres (5–10 gallons) per tonne.

Metamorphic Rocks

Metamorphic rocks form the third main group of rocks. Without practice, some may be hard to distinguish from igneous rocks. For an explanation of some of the terms used by geologists to describe their formation, textures and structures, see page 56.

Slate

Slate is a fine-grained, compact rock, formed by the low-grade regional metamorphism of shales and sometimes mudstones and tuffs. Slate splits readily into thin, parallel-sided sheets, which are used for roofing. But the sheets are usually at an angle to the original bedding planes. This is because the cleavage is formed by the realignment of minerals during metamorphism. The bedding planes can usually be seen, as can occasional, distorted fossils. The composition of slate varies according to the original (parent) rock, but mica and chlorite are important. As can be seen in the picture on this page, crystals of iron pyrites may grow in slate during metamorphism. Slate is often black or grey, but it also occurs in shades of blue, brown, buff and green.

Marble

Marble is a beautiful, easily-cut rock, which takes a high polish. The specimen on this page comes from Carrara, Italy. Carrara marble has been prized by great sculptors, such as Michelangelo. Snowy-white marble is most used in sculpture, but there are black, green, red and yellow varieties. The colour may be uniform, or patchy or banded.

A compact, granular rock with no cleavage, marble is formed by contact and regional metamorphism of limestone. It is medium to coarse-grained. In low-grade marbles, distorted fossils may be seen. But high temperatures destroy them. Marble consists chiefly of calcite or dolomite, with smaller amounts of other minerals.

Slate containing iron pyrites

Marble (Carrara, Italy)

Cordierite hornfels (Cumbria, England)

Mica schist (Scotland)

Quartzite (Korea)

Gneiss composed of
quartz and mica

Hornfels

Hornfels is the name for a group of contact metamorphic rocks. Varieties are named after the most significant minerals they contain. For example, two varieties are cordierite hornfels and andalusite hornfels. Hornfels is a tough, massive rock. It has no cleavage and is often fine-grained, although large grains of the dominant mineral often speckle the surface. It may be black, blue, green or grey.

Mica Schist

Schists are a group of medium to coarse-grained rocks formed by regional metamorphism, at lower temperatures than gneiss. Schists are named after the prominent minerals in them. They are cleavable, but the planes are rougher and more irregular than those in slate. The commonest parent rocks are mudstones and siltstones. They may be black, brown, pink or red. They are often coloured by the almandine variety of garnet.

Quartzite

This tough, medium-grained and even-textured rock is created by the contact and regional metamorphism of quartz sandstones. It consists mostly of quartz, but feldspar, mica and other minerals may occur in small amounts. It may be white, grey, reddish or yellowish. It is much harder than marble, which it may resemble.

Gneiss

Gneiss is the name for a group of medium to coarse-grained, grey or pink rocks, formed by high-grade regional metamorphism. The parent rock may be sedimentary or igneous, and feldspar, mica and quartz are common minerals. A feature of many gneisses is their irregular banding, caused by the separation of crystals of differing sizes and shades into alternating bands. But some gneisses are granular. When struck, gneisses break into blocks rather than plates.

Part of a stony-iron meteorite (with fayalite)

Rocks from Space

Between 1969 and 1972, American astronauts brought back samples of Moon rock. The Russians also contributed with their automatic Luna probes, which obtained soil samples. But geologists did not have to wait until the Space Age to study rocks from beyond Earth. Meteorites have been arriving since ancient times.

Meteorites

Meteorites are fragments of the debris left behind after the formation of the Solar System. Most fragments burn and break up when they reach the Earth's atmosphere and about 40 or 50 meteorites are found, on average, each year. There are three main kinds of meteorites. *Iron meteorites* consist chiefly of iron-nickel alloys. *Stony-iron meteorites* contain nickel-iron, with some silicate minerals. *Stony meteorites* are composed of silicates, notably olivine and pyroxene, with some plagioclase and a little nickel-iron. Most stony meteorites are chondrites, which contain small, round globules, called chondrules. But a few lack chondrules and are called achondrites.

The largest meteorites are iron meteorites. The largest is in Namibia, in south-west Africa. It weighs about 60 tonnes (59 long tons). Large meteorites strike the Earth with great force. The largest crater caused by a meteorite is Meteor Crater, in Arizona in the USA. This crater is about 1200 metres (about 4000 ft) wide and 180 metres (590 ft) deep.

You will be very lucky if you find a meteorite. Features to look for are chondrules or nickel-iron, and a fusion crust. This is a thin black crust, which is often on one side only of a meteorite. It was caused by intense heating during the meteorite's passage through the atmosphere.

Tektites

These small, glassy objects are concentrated in certain parts of the

Assorted tektites

Moon rock

world and they have local names. For example, those from Bohemia and Moravia in Europe are called moldavites; those from southern Australia are australites; and those from the southeast USA are bediasites and Georgia tektites. Nearly four-fifths of known tektites come from the Philippines. They are called philippinites.

Some scientists once thought that tektites were meteorites. But most scientists now think that they were formed by meteorite impacts on Earth. These impacts generate great heat which melts existing rock. Tektites are mostly between 1 and 3 cm (0·4–1·2 inches) across, but a few are larger. They are mostly black and are rich in silica and also in aluminium, lime and potash.

Moon Rock

Small samples of Moon rock are now in some museums. These rocks are igneous. No sedimentary rocks exist, because the Moon lacks both air and water and so there is no weathering. The youngest Moon rocks are about 3000 million years old. The oldest are about 4600 million years old, the same age as Earth. The younger rocks are in basins, or maria. The older rocks are in the highlands.

Scientists think that the oldest rocks are part of the original crust. But the Moon was later bombarded by meteorites. The bombardment reached its peak around 4000–3900 million years ago. As it declined, lava, similar to basaltic magma on Earth, spread over the floors of the basins. Volcanic activity ceased about 3000 million years ago, since then the Moon has been 'dead'. Moon dust is probably debris caused by meteorite impacts and glassy spheres occur. The highland regions of the Moon consist largely of anorthosite, which is an igneous rock containing a large proportion of plagioclase feldspar.

The geologist Harrison Schmitt was the first scientist to visit the Moon. He took part in the last mission of the Apollo project, in December 1972.

Index

ACKNOWLEDGMENTS

The author and publishers wish to thank the following for their kind help in supplying photographs for this book:

Australian News and Information Bureau 55; Australian Pearl Co. 40; British Museum 38; Bruce Coleman 8; Crown copyright reproduced with permission of the Controller of HM Stationery Office 15 right, 39; Diamond Information Bureau 17, 28, 43, 62 centre; Dinosaur National Monument 55 right; Institute of Geological Sciences 21, 27, 41, 48, 49 right, 60 left, 61 right, 63 bottom, 69 left, 73 bottom, 74 right, 89 top, 91 bottom, 92 bottom, 95 bottom right, 96 bottom, 97 centre three, 98 top, 116 top left, 122 centre and bottom; Middlesex Hospital 15 bottom; NASA 123; North Carolina Travel 42 left; Pat Morris 12, 15 top left, 18, 49 left, 54; Robert Harding Associates 19 left; Scottish Tourist Board 19 right; South African Tourist Corporation 24 left; United Kingdom Atomic Energy Authority 37; Zefa 47, 50. All other photographs supplied by Peter Green, Imitor.

The publishers wish to thank Professor D. T. Donovan and Ms Wendy Kirk of the University College of London Geology Department for making available the department's collection of minerals and rocks for photography.